P9-AFA-418

The Green Bench

A dialogue about leadership

and change

OTHER BOOKS BY MATT RAWLINS

Emails from Hell

The Green Bench II
More Dialogue about leadership
and communication

The Green Bench

A dialogue about leadership
and change

Matt Rawlins

Amuzement Publications
Salem, Oregon

Cover design by Lisa Bartsch

The Green Bench by Matt Rawlins.
Copyright © 1999 Matt Rawlins. All rights reserved. No part
of this publication may be reproduced, stored in a retrieval
system, or transmitted in any form or by any means -- elec-
tronic, mechanical, photocopy, recording, or any other --
except for brief quotations in printed reviews, without the
prior permission of the publisher.

Library of Congress Catalog Card Number: 00-190822

Acknowledgment

I have worked in a non-profit organization for many years. It is hard work and challenging at times. There are many leaders that have shown me much and modeled how to serve others. For their friendship and modeling I am deeply appreciative. Thank you Kel Steiner, Gary and Helen Stephens, Loren and Darleen Cunningham, Steve and Marie Goode, David and Carol Boyd and the countless others that have toiled with me to try and make this world a better place.

Dedication

When I was a child I received results from an IQ test that said I was "markedly below average." My father would not accept what the test declared. This book is dedicated to him who never doubted what it took me so long to find out.

Chapter One

DID YOU LEARN ANYTHING?

I do not know what I may appear to the world but to myself I seem to have been only a boy playing on the sea shore, and diverting myself by now and then finding a smoother pebble or a prettier shell than ordinary, whilst the great ocean of truth lay all undiscovered before me.
Isaac Newton

Experience is not what happens to a man.
It is what a man does with what happens to him.
Aldous Huxley

I have never let my schooling interfere
with my education.
Mark Twain

Once there was a man who was a wise manager. His co-workers looked up to him and trusted him. They knew they could ask difficult questions and he would listen. Each worker understood the meaning of the job and its importance in the overall picture. Each felt the challenge to take risks while enjoying the safety of office stability. They knew the importance of change and how to embrace it for growth.

But it hadn't always been that way.

As a young manager he could clearly remember sitting in his small cubicle wondering if he could keep up the pace. His monthly planner hung on the wall, looking like an adventure map with X's marking too many spots. His organizer lay open before him, with each day demanding its needs be met. The computerized office scheduler glared back at him, changing by the minute as others adjusted meetings times, places and agendas. He knew how to fill his schedule and he could prove his worth to the business by being as busy as anyone else. But he was tired of throwing his time at the problems that besieged him.. What he needed was wisdom. He knew his mind could work better. He knew he could be more effective. But he didn't know how, and with his education and experience it seemed absurd to ask.

As a boy, he could clearly remember his first years of school. The unspoken lessons he learned were:

- Don't ask too many questions. They will think you are a "slow learner" or just kissing up to the teacher.

- Do as you're told. Do your work the way the teacher wants it done, even if your way works better.

- Learning is not fun. Even though the hardest things in life (speaking, walking, reading) were learned with great fun by age seven. Education could only come through hard, painful work.

- Learning amounts to stuffing your mind with worthless information. You can forget it as quickly as you learn it.

- Compliance is rewarded, even if you didn't learn anything.

- Failure is punished, even if you learned cool things.

- Cheaters on Math tests prosper.

- You imagination has nothing to do with intelligence.

What he also learned was a system and how to get around in it. School, at its best, could be tolerated. At its worst, mind-numbing agony.

●●●

After public school standardized and homogenized him, "higher education" seized his brain and taught him about a new "system." He did some time at the local college and actually learned a few things, he survived just long enough to get his degree.

Formal schooling taught him one thing well: he just couldn't remember what it was.

He believed he had learned everything he needed to know. His learning days were done and he wanted to get into the real world. One thing he knew, his common sense and street smarts would take him a long way.

●●●

He started low on the "totem pole." It wasn't the greatest job, but he knew the only direction he could go was up. He found a classic car, rebuilt the engine, carefully picked out a new color for a paint job, put some new tires on it, and drove it around looking at the people who were going on to more school. He asked himself, *who was smarter*? The admiring looks of people as he drove by gave him his answer.

• • •

He worked hard. Months passed, and then years. He was right. He did move up. First it was a pay increase. Then benefits, and graveyard line supervisor. He jumped to a large company as a day-time supervisor and soon, painfully realized if he was going to go further he had to go back into the system. More school. He made it to assistant manager and stalled there while he scratched his way through to an MBA. The degree was a major withdrawal from his family life account, but he made it and moved up to a manager, but with each move he had to work harder just to keep up. He had always thought it was just a matter of giving it everything he had. He gave it everything he had, and realized it wasn't enough. It wasn't just physical work, street smarts and the technical information that school crammed in him; now he needed wisdom.

Wisdom to know:

> • How to survive change. . .sometimes major change. . like a company buyout...or loss of a huge client, account or contract.

> • How to know what questions to ask to get the information he really needed?

• How to help people with different skills, training and views of life, work and learn together?

• How to get at the core issues and resolve them?

All the answers were not black and white, simple, spit out the right reply, look it up and tell 'em what the book says, everyone oughta know, responses.

Instead they were gray, complex, changing, risky, no one remembers, don't know where to look, wanna hide, put 'em off, might lose your job, ask someone else, see me tomorrow, uncertainties.

Now he had to try to think for himself.

Then, to make matters worse, there was all this talk about learning organizations, smarter workers, downsizing the company and putting more responsibility on the workers.

It wasn't about hard work anymore.
It was about smart work.
It wasn't about education.
It was about thinking and learning.
It was also about security, comfort, confidence, wisdom, and his future. . .

What if everybody else — especially his boss — could see what he was feeling or hear his thoughts? Surely they could tell just by looking that he had weighed in and was out of his class. Was he going to be like a computer chip, quickly obsolete, pulled out and replaced by someone newer, quicker, smarter and better? Would his wife and children have to pay the price of his lack of wisdom? He knew he was in trouble. He knew he needed to learn. He had spent his whole life fitting into the system and now the system didn't help. Where did he go from here?

● ● ●

The young manager walked out of the Vice President's office with the words still ringing in his ears. "We brought you in to make a difference in this division. Things are getting tight and you better start to produce, or else!" The young manager didn't have to think hard to know what "or else" meant. He thought of the kids needing new clothes to keep up with the fads, the "new" house they just purchased as a celebration of this new job. He arrived at his desk and settled in. He looked again at the stack of papers in front of him. He stared at the phone messages and the "to do" list: reports due, decisions to be made, planning, problem solving, and people at every turn. How could he learn to deal with all these things and have them make sense? How could he give back to his family some of his precious time?

He didn't know the answer and his management "tools" couldn't help him now. He wasn't about to ask anyone in the office either. If they knew he didn't know, it would make it worse. He was *supposed* to know.

He quickly stood up, grabbed his coat and headed for the door.

●●●

Thankfully the secretary was on the phone so she couldn't ask where he was going and when he would be back. He didn't know either.

He headed for the park. The day was cool with large clouds rolling across the sky. The breeze cooled him.

He headed for a green bench under a large old oak tree. He settled himself on it and waited for his mind to settle as well.

The gentle moving of the bench caught his attention and he looked over to see who had invaded his private space. A gray-haired man in a dark blue sweater with khaki pants was settling down next to him, .

"Mind if I borrow a little of your bench for a while?" the older gentleman asked.

"Nope." He wished he'd had the guts to say, "Yes, I do mind. . ."

They sat in silence for a few minutes and then the old man spoke.

"Actually I think of this as my bench!" He turned soft blue eyes toward the young man. "I've come here often over these last months and kind of like the place. I was tempted to put a reserved sign on it. But I figured the city. . .or the kids. . .would rip it off."

"Yep," the young man muttered as he looked the other way.

The old man held out his hand and said, "My name is Marques, but my friends call me Q because they couldn't get used to the spelling of my name. Some of them also think I ask too many questions."

The young man slowly took his hand and said "Hi."

"So what do you do?" asked Q looking out over the water.

"I work in an office," replied the businessman. [Wishing the old man would go away,] but it wasn't working too well.

"What do you do in the office?"

"I'm a manager for a production team. So what about you, what do you do?" asked the young man hoping to get the focus off himself.

"Nothing actually. I just retired from teaching and have been thinking about what I want to do next. I have a few odd jobs, but mostly I'm just enjoying the days." Q sat up straight and tried to show how proud he was to be retired.

"They say retirement is supposed to be great."

He let out a deep breath and smiled as he leaned over towards the young man and whispered, "Retirement isn't all it's made out to be. Actually, it's kind of boring if the truth be known."

The young manager smiled in return. He figured an old retired teacher couldn't be that dangerous.

He was right, but in another way he was also very wrong.

• • •

Thus began an unusual friendship. A retired teacher who missed the relationship he had for years with his inquisitive students and a young manager who was willing to become an inquisitive student for the first time in his life.

• • •

Q turned and asked, "You seem to have something on your mind."

The young manager, in a brief moment of abandonment, shared with Q how his work with people, management, organization, planning, problem solving and leadership confused him. He couldn't afford to leave his job, and he didn't know how to accomplish his job. He felt blocked, even with all his education, it was as if he'd finally maxed out on what he could handle and do.

"That reminds me of a story," said Q nodding.

Oh no, thought the young manager. *Here we go.*

"Some scientists were studying a certain kind of fish. I think it was an Arawana, maybe from South America, but I am not sure. Anyway, they took this fish that ate smaller fish and put it in a tank. They put a glass divider down the middle of the tank, and put some smaller fish on the other side of the tank. The Arawana was hungry and saw those smaller fish and went after them like a hungry cat on a rat. "

Q looked inquiringly at the young manager to see if he was listening.

"Yeah, go ahead," he said.

"There was a problem for this large fish though, he kept running into the glass divider. He couldn't see the glass and would hit it whenever he tried to get at the fish. For a while he just kept hitting and hitting it. Slowly, with the passing of time, he tried less, as they seemed out of his reach. It wasn't too much longer before he just gave up."

"For reasons beyond him, the fish could not get what he wanted. A little while later the scientists removed the glass divider and let the fish swim wherever it wanted. The smaller fish were terrified of this huge new enemy swimming so close. But now the large fish just swam slowly around ignoring them.

"A day or two went by and the big fish finally died."

Q was silent for a moment and then leaned over close to the young manager and asked, "Why do you think the fish died?"

The young manager resisted the temptation to roll his eyes. Smartly, he answered, "Uhh, starvation!"

Q smiled and looked back at the young manager and asked, "But he had lots of food all around him, didn't he?"

The young manager nodded, playing the game.

"No, it wasn't starvation. He died from experience."

"What are you talking about?" Okay, so the old guy had his attention.

Q continued, "The fish had tried to eat the others many times. Once he made up his mind what he could and couldn't do, he didn't try again. His past experiences dictated his present decisions. So he stopped growing and learning. As a result, he kicked the bucket."

The young manager was thinking, *What's your point?*

Q let the young manager think.

The young manager thought back to what he had learned in school, he saw faces of friends laughing at him, average grades, lists of words to memorize, abstract formulas and boring teachers. . .

Q invaded his thoughts and said, "You're not dead yet. But you might be pretty close."

The young manager startled. Then he let his head sag, not sure what to say.

Q drew his arm back and spotted an open spot by the young manager's ribs. He let his elbow fly.

The young manager was so startled he almost fell off the bench.

"Ouch, that hurt," he objected.

"Dead men don't feel pain. Remember I said you're not dead YET!" Q laughed.

The young manager began to smile as understanding seeped in.

"So you are saying that I am stuck in how I do things. That being stuck is killing me!"

"Good!" said Q. He leaned forward and asked, "Mind if I tell you about one of my students?"

"No, go ahead," replied the young manager, not knowing what kind of story to expect this time.

"Years ago I had this little guy in my class. He sat in the front row on the edge of his seat. Any time I asked a question his hand would shoot up, like it was spring loaded."

Q sat on the edge of the bench like the little boy.

"Like this," he said, raising his hand.

The young manager laughed at this old teacher sitting on the edge of a green park bench shooting his hand in the air.

Q looked over at the young man and said, "You sit on the edge of the bench and shoot your hand up like that little boy did. I want to see you do it.

"Come on, I'll wait for you."

The young manager smiled and slowly did it.

Q said, "He was much faster than that, but you got the idea."

The young manager decided he wouldn't laugh at the old teacher any more.

Q continued, "I mean, I only had to think of a question and before I could get it out of my mouth, He would shoot his hand into the air, waving it to make sure I saw him."

"When I called on him he would sit there for a second and then blurt out any thought that happened to be in his mind. He didn't know the real answer most of the time, but that didn't stop him. He thought students needed to know all the answers, so he was going to give me an answer, no matter what the question. I could have asked about nuclear fusion, Napoleon, numerology, you think of a question and this little boy had an answer."

Q paused and looked over at the young manager and said, "I know a lot of people like that young boy. They think they have to have all the answers. They don't care what the question is, they have to have an answer. They think because they attended school and swallowed some predigested information thrown to them that they should have all the answers.

"I have far more questions now than I ever had. Give me someone who knows how to ask a good question. Now that is someone who wants to really live."

The young manager looked wide-eyed.

"Really? You still have questions? I mean, you will admit you have questions?"

Q nodded and said, "Questions are the only thing that keeps me going. Albert Einstein said 'The important thing is not to stop questioning. Curiosity has its own reason for existing. One cannot help but be in awe when he contemplates the mysteries of eternity, of life, of the marvelous structure of reality. It is enough if one tries merely to comprehend a little of this mystery every day. Never lose a holy curiosity.' The way I see it, if you don't have questions, you aren't alive. One of the biggest killers for people is the idea that you have to know everything and that something is wrong with you if you don't.

He let the thought sink in for a second and then began again.

"Mind if I ask you a question?"

The young manager shook his head.

"When you don't know an answer to a question or a situation, how do you feel?"

The young manager thought about recent experiences. He thought of his education and now his new job with all the expectations from others and himself of what he 'should know.'

"Well, I feel incompetent, like I should know the answer and that something is wrong with me if I don't. Even when there is no reason why I should know the answer. I feel dumb that I don't know the answer."

Q looked over at his young student shaking his head slowly and said, "That little lie causes more suffering each year than any disease."

A few moments passed and Q pulled a piece of paper out of his pocket, leaned back and said with a hint of hope, A researcher named Laing wrote:

There is something I don't know
that I am supposed to know.
I don't know what it is I don't know,
and yet am supposed to know,
And I feel I look stupid
if I seem both not to know it
and not know what it is I don't know.

Therefore, I pretend I know it.
This is nerve-wracking
since I don't know what I must pretend to know.
Therefore I pretend to know everything.

I feel you know what I am supposed to know
but you can't tell me what it is
because you don't know that I don't know what it is.

You may know what I don't know, but not
that I don't know it, and I can't tell you. So you will
have to tell me everything ." [1]

"That's how I feel," admitted the young manager.

Q shook his head, "Welcome to the human race," he said "I wish I had a penny for every time people felt that way. I wish I had a penny for each time I felt that way!"

The young manager mumbled agreement.

Q reached into his pocket and pulled out his wallet. I have a card I have put my key thoughts about learning on that might help you in your office.

The young manager reached out to take it and look at it.

Q hesitated, and said, "On second thought, let's not look at it and see what happens for a while. I will show it to you later."

"I would like to see it now," the young manager said.

"I put these together as reminders for me in working with my students at school. Let's wait and see how it will fit in the business world," Q responded.

"OK, I will wait for a while but I would like to see them."

"You will get to see it later."

They sat for a while before the young manager looked at his watch and realized he had to get back to work.

He stood up and said to Q, "Thanks, I needed that. I hope to see you again."

Q responded, "Glad I could help. I'm out here every Tuesday after I visit my mother, if you have any more questions."

"I'll remember that," the young manager responded as he headed off for the office.

As the young manager walked back he wondered what his life would be like if he could learn to accept that he didn't have to know everything and it was a good thing to ask questions. He thought about his new job and realized he didn't even know what the questions were he should be asking. He decided he would find out.

LEARNING STARTS:

<u>When we stop pretending we know everything.</u>
"I'm sorry, I don't understand. Could you say that again?" "I don't know." "I never thought of that, it's a great idea!"

<u>When we allow ourselves freedom to ask questions.</u>
"What did you mean?" "How does that work?" "That still doesn't make sense, could you take it a little slower and walk me through it?"

<u>When we are more interested in learning than in what people think about us not knowing</u>.
We are born to learn. It is as easy and natural as breathing. The effects of not breathing and not learning are the same.

<u>When hurtful experiences that would stop us from learning are left in the past</u>.
When comments like: "Are you stupid or what?" "You sure are slow, anyone can do that!" "You blew it again." "You aren't ever going to get this, you might as well give up!" "This doesn't seem to be your area, why don't you try something else!" "Can't you do anything right?" are finally buried and laid to rest.

Chapter Two

IF I'M NOT DEAD YET, HOW DO I GET UNSTUCK?

Nothing is permanent but change.
Heraclitus

We live in a moment of history where change is so speeded up that we begin to see the present only when it is already disappearing.
R. D. Laing

Q's words floated in the young manager's mind like the words on a sign pulled behind a small plane.

'You're not dead, YET.'

He spoke to himself, 'Pain is good; it's a sign I am still alive.'

The young manager thought it over as he drove home. *I have thought education means I have to have all the answers. Maybe all it means is that I should know how to ask better questions. Maybe learning is different from education and I can learn while I am at work. Now, I am also going to accept the harsh reality* -- anyone watching him would have seen him smiling to himself -- *that I don't have to know everything.*

It was so simple he kept wondering why he hadn't thought of it himself. His eyes seemed to see everything in a new way. Feelings he hadn't felt in years came creeping back. He remembered questions he asked his father years ago. *'Why is it like that dad? How...? Who...? What...?'* Thoughts stirred him, *there is a special wonder about not knowing something. A joy in exploring. Allowing yourself not to know is like becoming a child again in some ways.*

Days went by and the young manager found himself looking out the office window to the little green bench below, just in case his new friend was there. It was empty.

"Excuse me," came a reply behind him.

He turned to see one of his production team and said, "Yes?"

"We just got the figures off the line and it is down 5%. What should we do?"

The young manager held his typical response and looked away. He finally turned back and said, "I don't know. Do you have any suggestions?"

The person from the production line looked around and then stared at the floor. Her hands started to crumble a paper and her feet started shuffling.

"It's okay," he said, "I do have some ideas, but I really don't know the cause. Let's ask around and see what we can find out."

The young manager paused, and then turned to explore.

Tuesday came and the day went by and still the bench was empty. He paused there for a moment and thought about his changing vocabulary. *"It must. . ."*, *moved towards "It could. . .", "I know. . .", allowed room for "What if. . .", "There is. . ." gave space to "Let's find. . ."*.

An office friend patted him on the back and asked, "What's the smile for? I haven't seen one on your face for a while."

The young manager, not even aware that he was smiling and caught off guard, mumbled about "not knowing," and went to finish some last minute details.

The day quickly ended. The young manager put on his coat and went out the front door for the drive home.

As he walked out the door he saw Q just sitting down on the little green bench.

He walked over and sat down next to him. "Mind if I borrow a little of your bench for a while?"

"I guess not!" came back a soft chuckling reply.

"I've been doing some thinking, and I wouldn't mind asking you for some help, if you don't mind." The young manager started right in, ready to talk with someone about his new thoughts.

Q smiled and listened.

"I've found that I can ask questions and begin to explore and learn again. But when I open myself up I realize I don't know as much as my degrees and I convinced myself I did."

Q nodded his head in understanding and the young manager continued.

"When this realization hit me, I also sensed I am going to have to change the way I do things, and in the end, I am not sure how to deal with change."

A breeze blew and Q looked long at the world around them.

"Look out there and tell me what you see?" were the words he finally stated.

The young manager looked over the water and then at the trees. He noticed some birds and responded. "I see some water, trees and some birds. I guess I don't get what you mean!"

"Look again, but look with eyes that are looking for things that are changing," came the slow gentle response.

The young manager settled onto the bench and tried to get comfortable. He looked out over the water and just watched it for a minute.

"Change, huh?" he muttered as he watched the water.

A breeze picked up again and the water on the lake began to ripple and form small waves. The ripples caught the young manager's eyes. He turned and said with a wrinkled brow and a long face, "The lake is changing. It was flat and calm, now it has small waves."

Q smiled and said with encouragement, "That's a start, you're on track. Keep looking."

The young manager shifted his position and continued to look around him.

Some leaves wrestled with the wind and lost, ending up in the lake.

Birds rode the wind like a surfer on a wave.

A young boy stood on the shore and fired rocks like miniature bombs into the lake.

The sun played peek-a-boo with the earth, dashing between the clouds rolling past. Seemingly it seemed to whisper, 'Now you see me, now you don't.'

The young manager's eyes grew large and he realized what was happening. He turned to Q and declared, "Everything is changing!

"The birds change their flight to com-pensate for the wind. The lake grows smaller when the rocks the little boy throws settle to the bottom. The leaves will move with the water and settle on a shore or be blown across it..."

"Change is going on all around us," Q interjected, "It just happens so subtly that we fail to see it."

"If change is going on all around and is so normal, why is it so difficult for me sometimes?" the young manager asked.

"Good question, you are learning quickly.

"Maybe that should wait for another day. You have enough to think about for now. Go and look for change and just watch."

LEARNING SEES:

Change is going on all around.
      There is a time and season for everything: a time to create and a time to conform; a time to invest and a time to sell; a time to bury and a time to raise it back to life; a time to tear down and a time to build; a time to grieve and a time to rejoice; a time to do research and a time to market; a time to search and a time to give up; a time to do it the way it's always been done and a time to forget how things have been done; a time to be silent and a time to speak; a time to applaud and a time to rebuke; a time to gather the troops and a time to disperse them.

Change is a normal part of life.
      Imagine a world that could not change. Change is linked directly to growth. The two are inseparatble.

Chapter Three

IF CHANGE IS NORMAL, WHY DOES IT HURT?

"Minds differ still more than faces."
Voltaire

"The harder you work, the harder
it is to surrender."
Vince Lombardi

The young manager was looking around like a child with his first pair of glasses. There was change going on everywhere. Such a simple thought had opened up such a wide door for him.

When one of the staff was sick and stayed home, it changed the flavor of the office. Another had a project due and rushed about to finish. Someone else had just finished a project and was relaxing, talking to a co-worker. Each day was different; it was a new day every day. Every moment was full of change.

He strolled down the hall watching all those around him. His mind shifted to his office. He just added a new secretary and he looked forward to the extra help. He turned into his office, only to find his new help had arrived early. She was hovering over his desk organizing it and putting all the papers in piles.

He quickly raised his voice and said, "Wait, don't change that, I won't know where anything is!"

He had no sooner settled that problem then someone walked in with an overnight package marked urgent. He opened the box up only to find new changes required in assembly. He sighed loudly and leaned back in his chair. "Change isn't all it's made out to be," he mumbled. "Where is Q? I have to understand this change thing better."

Now that he was looking for change, he saw it everywhere. In fact, change seemed to be at the core of some of his greatest frustrations.

Tuesday rolled around and he walked out the front doors into a windy, cool day and headed over to the green bench. A young couple, deep in conversation, had already claimed the bench. He stopped and stared for a minute and then walked over to the rail and looked around.

Q was coming slowly down the path, watching everything going on around him. He looked at the young couple and then back to the young manager. "I see we are confronted with change right away!" remarked Q as he drew near.

With a week of frustrations built up, the young manager started with a question, "Why am I bothered with change? If it is so normal, how come it's such a pain?"

The young couple stood as if on cue and moved, arm in arm, down the path.

Q and the young manager walked over to the green bench and sat down.

"Change is wonderful, yet it can be painful at times," came Q's response after they settled on the bench.

"I remember in one of my classes, I was feeling rather bored. I arrived at school a little early and decided to move all the desks around. Well, it came time for the class to start. The bell rang and they dragged themselves in. You wouldn't believe the look on their faces. You would have thought they were on a differ-

ent planet. They couldn't believe what someone had done to 'their' seats. We had a great
discussion about change that morning."

Q smiled as he thought of all those kids
and continued, "There are two parts to this that
are important to understand. They are both
linked to our uniqueness as humans. The first
is the result of the way our brain works. The
second has to do with losing part of ourselves
when we change."

Q hesitated for a second and looked at
the young manager. The young manager felt
like he needed to respond in some way as Q
seemed to look into his heart and see the question lurking there.

"I am not sure what you mean. What
does that have to do with my office and managing?"

Q smiled and said, "It has everything to
do with your office and managing, trust me.
They're really simple and we will take them
one at a time.

"The brain is an amazing piece of art
work that we are only just beginning to understand. In essence, it's an open system that has
different components constantly interacting
with each other, and based on that interaction,
the system changes."

"Whoa!" said the young manager shaking his head. "I thought you said it was
simple!" The young manager coughed and
made a distorted face, "I feel like I am back in
school."

"Hey, what's wrong with being in school?" Q asked mockingly defending his home turf.

"Oops, s-o-r-r-y," the young manager said drawing out the sorry for several seconds.

"I will try to make this as simple as possible," Q responded, throwing his hands in the air.

Q pulled out a cup of Jell-O from his paper sack.

"This Jell-O," he said, holding up the little white cup, "is like our brain. Not exactly a compliment, but I guess it'll work."

He opened up his thermos and said, "What happens if I pour a drop of this hot coffee onto the top of the Jell-O?"

The young manager stated the obvious, "The Jell-O will melt where the coffee lands."

"Right," Q said as he tipped a drop of coffee onto the Jell-O. They both looked at it as Q took out a tissue and blotted out the little bit of coffee so they could see what had happened clearly.

"What if I released another drop right next to this one?"

The young manager looked at the first impression already made from the first drop and said, "The coffee will run into the other little spot where the other drop hit and there is now a little depression."

The teacher nodded his head in approval and went on, "So you could say that the Jell-O changed after the first drop and reacted a little differently with the second drop."

The young manager repeated what he just heard, "The first drop affected the Jell-O and so when the second drop came it would react a little differently from the first because the Jell-O had changed."

"That's right!" said the teacher, "Another drop or two next to these and you would have the beginnings of a little stream or channel."

Q hesitated a second and then looked over at the young manager with a smile and a twinkle in his eyes, "What would happen if I changed the order of the drops and where they landed?"

The young manager thought for a second and then drew circles in the dirt and asked as he pointed. "You mean if you drew them in a different order. Then it wouldn't form a stream but just an odd collection of impressions waiting for other drops to come along to form a different pattern."

"Yes," came bursting forth as Q saw his young student understand. He then continued, "So the heat of the drops, their size, the order they come, where they land, what has happened before, if there was fruit in the Jell-O, would all have an impact on how the coffee and the Jell-O interact."

"I'm following you," the young manager said as he nodded his head.

"Now," Q continued, "if you can think of the hot coffee as input into our lives, things like books read, types of relationships, family life, accidents, and so forth, and our brains like the Jell-O you can understand how a human brain works. Learning is not only about gathering information, it involves everything that happens to us. Emotions are critical to the organization in our mind. Emotions and reasoning interact and cannot be separated. Although we all have the same set of systems, including our senses and basic emotions, they are integrated a little differently in every brain. Learning actually changes the structure of the brain. The more we learn, the more unique we become. Each brain is a unique self-organizing system."

Q took a deep breath and sat back.

"Each person is totally unique," he whispered, "Our brains are such a beautiful creation." He leaned forward and with a slow deep voice said, "Did you know there are about one hundred billion nerve cells in the brain, and in a single human brain the number of possible interconnections between these cells is greater than the number of atoms in the universe? As the brain processes information and reacts to new experiences it literally creates new channels and changes. [2] These modifications will then influence how it will react with new stimuli that is taken in as input. The input will form patterns that will in turn reinforce our own unique mental map."

The young manager sat back, thinking.

Q beamed at the splendor of it all and said, "Now, back to your question. The first part of the answer to why change is so hard. God knew we would have a limited amount of strength. With that in mind, he made us so that once we have invested our energy in a choice, we don't have to use more energy all over again on the same choice. The decision process leaves an impression or mark on our mind. The next time we are confronted with the same or a similar choice, we have a pattern, already begun in our mind.

As time passes, these choices settle into habits for us and this provides us with stability. Without these patterns we would have no sense of history and part of our identity would be lost. Can you imagine the energy needed to remake all the decisions that face us every day? If we had to remake every decision anew, each day, we would be in terrible shape. I heard of a man who, because of a World War II accident, has only a five-minute memory for anything occurring to him. He's constantly relearning reality. Every face he meets is a new face, even those who care for him daily; every experience is a new experience. Without a mind that created patterns and remembered them, we would all end up that way."

Q reached out and put his hand on the young manager's shoulder and said, "When you are asked or challenged to do something new, you literally have to change the maps or patterns of your mind, which is hard work. Once the patterns have been set, it is always more difficult to change them, then to just keep going the same old way."

"I get tired just thinking about all that work my brain does. No wonder change can be unsettling and difficult," the young manager said.

Q smiled and said, "I remember one little girl. She had to have everything just right. If you tried to change anything once it was set up and organized, she would go at you like a cornered cat."

Q leaned over and said reverently, "Her brain made deep channels very quickly!"

The young manager smiled as he stood up to leave, "What was her name? I think she and her family are working in my office."

LEARNING EMBRACES:

Each individual as unique.
     Each worker brings a unique mind to work with them. This "mind map" is made up of abilities and talents given by God at birth and things they have learned or experienced in their lives. Nobody will do things the exact same way you do. Everyone's map is different.

Doing things over and over creates patterns for how we like to have things done.
     The first time you do something (or allow others to do something) is very important. It will more than likely be repeated in the future, getting easier each time. Ask yourself before you do something the first time, "Do I want this duplicated in my work or team in the weeks, months and years to come?" The first process of how something is done will create a pattern for how others following you will do it.

You can change the map, but it is difficult work.
     Patterns form habits over time that make life much easier for us. Remember, when you want to change something, anything, it will force people to change their "minds" and make them work harder until the new way is formed. Is the change worth the cost?
     This is also why looking at things from a different perspective can be difficult sometimes. We literally have to change our mind to see things in a new way.

Chapter Four

WHAT KEEPS ME FROM GETTING STUCK?

*"We are half ruined by conformity,
but we should be wholly ruined without it."*
Charles Dudley Warner

*"Courage is resistance to fear, mastery of fear — not
absence of fear. Except a creature be part coward it
is not a compliment to say it is brave."*
Mark Twain

*Some people walk carefully through life, so
they can arrive safely at death's door.*

*When we risk being ourselves, it is the
greatest act of creativity and an
expression on vulnerability.*

The young manager started the new day at work and tried to settle in. There was a stack of paper to deal with, calls to make, and people to meet. Each situation could be different depending on what he said, where they met, earlier events in the day or a thousand different variables all interacting. Based then on those interactions everything could change. Yet there would be patterns that would stay the same every day. He watched the sales manager walk in with his hot coffee and fresh donut in her hand. It was the same for her every morning.

He took a deep breath and relaxed. Culture, mental maps, what a wonderful help they were. He gave a quick thanks for these maps that meant he could give and expect the same basic responses from people on any given day, as they would usually be true to their mental maps.

He worked through the morning and then realized it was lunch time. Actually, the growling of his stomach and images of Jell-O, set his mind to thinking of where he should go for lunch.

All the old places sounded boring and for some odd reason he wanted to try something new.

He thought to himself. *If my mental maps influence me to do things the same way, why do I want to try something new?*

He decided to ask his teacher.

●●●

A week slipped by and the young manager saw Q sitting on a bench farther down the walkway. He smiled and went out to talk with him.

"So, if we are such creatures of habit, how come you moved to a new bench?" the young manager asked slyly, thinking he had caught him.

Q sat enjoying the sun. "Watch this," he said as he reached into a bag and pulled out a handful of pigeon food and then held his palm open.

A small flock of pigeons swarmed around his hand and settled on every available inch. They furiously attacked the food with little specks of it flying everywhere. A huge white and gray spot suddenly appeared on Q's pants. He moaned and shooed the birds away and threw the rest of the feed on the path. The young manager broke out laughing.

Q found his handkerchief and tried to clean up the mineral deposit and then quickly said, "I'm glad you noticed I'm at a new bench," Q smiled. "God has not left us bound to our habits or mental maps. They're good reference points but he knew we would need some help or we would get stuck."

"And what help did He provide for us?" asked the young manager, trying to figure out what it could be.

Q leaned forward and whispered to him, "Do you know the difference between a rut and a grave?"

The young manager shook his head.

"Their dimensions," Q snorted loudly with laughter, "A rut is just a grave with no end in sight!"

After a few more chuckles he settled down and continued, "God put in the heart of each person a desire for risk, creativity, challenge, adventure, for new and different things. It is a natural part of everyone's life.

"Risk is that attraction that keeps us alive and moving. God didn't want us to get stuck, so he put within each of us a desire for novelty, a desire to be creative, a hunger to see beyond ourselves, an urge to keep us listening for more. Its strength will vary, it may be hidden under deep hurts, it may respond to different opportunities, but it is within the heart of all humans."

Q reached over and picked a dandelion and continued, "Why do you think people chase the lottery, or get hooked on gambling, climb the highest mountains, or just desire to go to a different restaurant? We know there is more, and we want to find a way to reach out and find it. Each one of us interprets this a little differently, but this desire for more is what can keep us from getting stuck in ruts.

He paused, then said, "When we keep risk in tension with our traditions, we can lead a full life.

"Oh dear, I am talking at you again aren't I?" chuckled the teacher. "I must not wear out my favorite pupil. Let me give you a practical example."

Q pulled the young manager up and started walking down the path with him.

"It's like walking. Risk is one foot and our patterns or traditions is the other. It is the tension of these two working together that keep us moving. As you walk, there's a split second when the weight is shifting from one foot to the other and we are off balance. So I guess you could say growth is a matter of momentary imbalance created by the tension between traditions and risk."

The young manager analyzed walking for the first time in his life. He felt his left leg going forward and his right going backward. He lifted his right leg and thought he felt it for a brief moment. A second of imbalance. He felt the movement in his steps over and over and began to be aware how true it was. Just as he was catching on to exactly when the imbalance was, the teacher extended his foot over and tapped his foot at that key moment and the young manager stumbled.

The young manager turned and looked at the teacher for a second with a big smile on his face. "I know, I know," the young manager said, "Imbalance is risky business."

The teacher reached out and lightly punched the young student's shoulder, "That was an illustration I just couldn't pass up."

He continued, "A lot of people talk about balance but that is not what I am saying. Our goal is not balance. The best balance we have is when we are not walking at all but standing still or sitting down. Many people are very balanced, and very dead. The key is tension or keeping the two working with each other. As long as there is tension, there is growth, movement and life. When the tension is lost you are either bound by traditions with no new life flowing through you, or addicted to risk with no stability, sense of history or identity.

"The area where most of us struggle is this area of risk. We must remember that no significant area of life is free from risk. It is a key ingredient in every accomplishment and every relationship. Whenever a decision is required, there is risk. Wherever there is intimacy, there is risk. Wherever people are succeeding, there is risk."3

Q stopped walking and watched a young boy shoot past them on his roller blades, "Did you know the Chinese character for risk can also be translated as 'dangerous opportunity'?"

He started walking again, "Let me ask you a question. What is there about risk, I'm not just talking about walking now, but as it relates to your work that makes stepping out a little scary?"

They walked quietly as the young manager looked back into the last few months

52

to see what he found within himself when there was an opportunity for risk.

"I guess, for me, the part that scares me, is, uh, the possibility of being wrong or not knowing."

He hesitated, "I guess if I were to be really honest, I am afraid of failure and rejection."

Q's eyes softened and grew moist. He gently reached over and placed his hand on the young manager's shoulder and whispered, "May I commend you on your honesty with yourself and me. I do not take that lightly."

They walked a couple of steps and Q continued, "True learning makes us vulnerable. All humans hunger for openness and yet the pain or fear of rejection is enough to make even the strongest soul run for cover.

"Even though I have tried to live a risky life, it is still hard work to be vulnerable with others."

Q looked over at the young manager and said, "It is wonderfully fulfilling when we let traditions and creativity work together. Sadly there are those who refuse to take a risk and become vulnerable. They end up dead on the inside and cynics on the outside. Like our fish that died from its experiences."

Q took a slow breath and continued, "Daniel Taylor said, 'Cynicism is both foolish and cowardly. Foolish because it under estimates the God-given human potential for overcoming pain, and cowardly because it is afraid to risk anything in the human adventure. The cynical spirit, like many others, insists on control or certainty before it will act and, lacking that, retreats into the false security of denial and defeat.'"

Q slowly shook his head. "Risk," he declared, "is indispensable to a significant life."

The young manager thought for a couple of minutes and then said, "Life doesn't leave you much choice, does it? I mean, you either die from boredom, become a cynic, or take a chance and step out when the moment is right."

He hesitated, "But then again, maybe there never is a right moment for risk. And that is what everyone is waiting for: the perfectly safe risk," the young manager said, laughing to himself.

Q joined his laughter and said, "I like that. Everyone is waiting for the perfectly safe risk."

So the young manager returned to work, afraid of the risks ahead and yet excited at what they might bring.

LEARNING KNOWS:

<u>Each individual is unique; therefore, as each
person embraces the vulnerability of being
himself there is a risk involved.</u>

Part of our uniqueness will be expressed
in how we learn. You can gather information
about something without being vulnerable, but
you cannot learn something until you take the
risk and become vulnerable.

<u>Creativity (being vulnerable equals risk) is as
important as traditions.</u> <u>Risk is a normal part of
life.</u>

Most managers wait until they're forced
by the economy, government, shareholders or
an employee uprising to take a risk. (Then at
least they have someone else to blame.) In
these times, it is often too late, and there is a lot
of threat and very little space for learning. Risk
must be a part of a disciplined life. Risk is not
baring your soul to your employees, it is simply managing from your heart as well as your
head.

Definition of a riskless manager: One who only
makes decisions by sticking closely to the last
decision on the issue and then makes only
slight changes to take care of the most urgent
aspects of the problem currently at hand.

Chapter Five

IS CHANGE THE BEGINNING
OR THE END?

*"I tell you the truth, unless a kernel of wheat falls to
the ground and dies, it remains only a single seed.
But if it dies, it produces many seeds."*
John 12:24

*"If I am a field that contains nothing but grass-
seed, I cannot produce wheat. Cutting the grass
may keep it short: but I shall still produce grass and
no wheat. If I want to produce wheat, the change
must go deeper than the surface. I must be ploughed
up and re-sown."*
C. S. Lewis

*All changes, even the most longed for, have their
melancholy; For what we leave behind us is a part of
ourselves; we must die
to one life before we can enter another.*
Anatole France

*The important thing is this: To be able at any
moment to sacrifice
what we are for what we could become*
Charles Dubois

The young manager started off the week by nervously calling his team together. They filed in and sat down in their usual seats. He took a deep breath and began, "I realize that some of the ways we do things around here may not be the most effective way. I have been reluctant to take risks and try changes, as many of you know. I am asking for your help. I want to take an opportunity and explore ideas of how we can change things to make life a little easier. I want to take it slowly as I think doing things the normal way provides stability for us, but I also want to explore what needs to change."

The young manager threw out the first idea, tentatively, then someone else threw out an idea and soon a good discussion was fired up. It felt dangerous and fulfilling at the same time.

A day passed and the young manager headed out of the office and down to his favorite green bench. He was really looking forward to a few moments of relaxing and talking with Q. He walked out the door into the bright sunshine and saw someone else sitting on his bench. He hesitated for a second and then walked on down the walkway. After a few minutes he saw his teacher sitting on another bench waiting for him.

He realized he would have never found him today if he had not moved on past his old bench. He smiled to himself and hurried over and sat down.

"I have been trying to put into practice what we have been talking about," the young manager started off.

"I can see that or you would not have found me here."

"I realized that just because things were always done a certain way, that did not mean they always had to be done that way. I felt there were better ways to organize the team, and I understand now, that I didn't want to take the risk, so I hid behind doing things the old way. I have to admit I was apprehensive but I got the team together and we talked about it for the first time. I also realized for the first time that they were waiting for me to take the risk and until I did, no one under me would. It's exciting as I realized how much I needed take the risk and make some changes. Thanks for your help," the young manager said.

The old teacher glowed, "You have found me at a new bench. You have also found a new part of yourself."

The young manager gave Q a long look and said, "You said there were two parts to change; I understand the first one better in that mental maps or patterns are formed in us that free us to do things without so much work, but I don't remember the second one."

Q watched the sun reflecting off the small waves in the water, the pond looked like a stage, full of dancing mirrors pushing the light in every direction. He was mesmerized, drinking in the beauty all around.

He broke free from the revelry and said, "The second area that makes change difficult for us is when we decide to change something, a part of ourselves must be willing to die."

"I thought you said something like that the other day, but then I was thinking I must have heard you wrong. This doesn't sound very exciting."

Q laughed, "Hear me out please, you haven't heard the whole story."

"OK, I'm all ears," the young manager said, cupping his hands behind his ears.

"Good, When God created us, he made us in a very special way. He gave us a gift that no other animal has. This present is the ability to freely embrace whatever we want to."

Q chuckled and added, "This can be good or it can be bad. Which reminds me of the time I took a young class of students to the zoo. We were walking around and came to the lions and tigers. One of the little girls - she must have had a stuffed tiger or cats at home - walked up to me and said, 'I love cats; can I go inside and play with them and hug them?

"I tried not to laugh and explained to her these were big cats and they liked to be left alone. I decided I had better keep an eye on that little girl during the rest of our time at the zoo!"

The young manager laughed and Q continued. "As I said, this gift can be good or bad, depending on how we use it. Let me try and illustrate this for you."

Q reached into his pocket, pulled out a battery, and held it in his hand.

"What is this used for?" Q asked the young manager.

"To run things, Walkmans, radios, lots of different things."

"Good. What happens when you use it for awhile?"

"I guess it runs out of power," responded the young manager, hoping the obvious was right.

"Right. We are like this battery, only we have freedom to do what we want with our energy. The problem is we only have so much energy or strength available to us before we start to run down. Our energy is the most vital part of us. It is our life. This strength is what allows us to do anything we do, and we must spend it wisely. God knew this could be a dilemma for us, so he gave us some help. He put within each of us a simple permanent reference point. It is an unwritten law of human nature and it's simply this: whatever we spend our energy on must have perceived value."

Q pulled out a penny and a quarter from his pocket. He held out his hand and showed them to the young manager. "You have a choice to select either one of these coins. You can only choose one. Which would you choose?"

"This is a breeze. I would take the quarter!" responded the young manager pleased that it seemed an obvious choice.

Q nodded his head, "Right, the quarter has greater value. When you recognize a greater value over a lesser value and a choice is needed, you will always choose the greater perceived value. It is the 'obvious' choice."

"This reference point is what allows us to safeguard our energy. Once we understand an object's value, we know how to respond. Seeing the value, makes the choice clear so we don't run around like a chicken with its head cut off trying to figure out what we should do next."

The teacher laughed and added, "If I may interrupt with a story again? Years ago, as class was starting, one of the boys came up to me and said, 'Do you know what a chicken looks like with its head cut off?'

I answered 'No.'

So he said, 'Yesterday afternoon Dad and I went out and had to kill some of our chickens and I saw what happens. I thought they would just fall over, but they don't. You should have seen them, here, I'll show you.'"

Q had a smile all over his face and leaned over and said to the young manager, "This student laid down on the ground and started flapping and hopping wildly all over the place. The other children saw it and decided they needed to join in. Just when all these kids were frantically hopping and jumping all over the place, the principal happened to be walking by and looked in. I just waved to him and pretended nothing unusual was happening."

"The principal stared for a couple of seconds and decided he didn't want to know what was going on and left. By this time I was enjoying it so much I decided I had better try, and I started to hop and flap all over the place. We had a great time.

"Funny thing is," laughed Q, "I stopped in at one of the older students' dances later that week, and it looked just like my students doing the dead chicken flop."

By this time, both men were laughing too hard to continue talking.

Finally they calmed down and Q started again, "Let's see, where were we? Oh, yes, how a reference point helps us. The choices we make, represents our life. These choices are simply an expression of our identity, who we are to others and ourselves. The longer we have chosen something, the greater the investment of ourselves in it, the more it becomes a part of us, and the harder it is to give it up.

"Change means that the part of our life we have invested in that area, and the security we have received from the choices made, must be given up. Learning means allowing our identity to unfold in unique, valuable, and sometimes sacrificial choices. Or in other words, in the change process, we must let that part of ourselves die."

"In small areas this may not be to difficult, but in the bigger areas this is where we get into problems."

The sun broke through again and the light dancing off the water continued.

"Do you understand what I mean?"

The young manager thought for a few moments and then tried to put the ideas into his own words.

"The more choices we make in a direction, the more we put our heart or energy into it. The more we express ourselves by those choices, the harder it is to give it up. To the degree we have invested our energy in choices, more of us dies when we have to change. That is why change can be so hard."

"That's right. We all have a unique identity, and we want to know that who we are will continue to live on,"

"When we make a choice, it creates an experience. That experience, when pleasant, is what draws us back to make the choice again. When I give up that choice or experience for something new, I have to be willing to give up that part of myself that is linked to it. It's again a little bit of a death of myself."

Q saw a look of concern on the young manager's face and said, "This may sound depressing, but it really isn't. That was the challenging part. There is an exciting part to this."

The young manager smiled as he could almost see an idea forming on Q's face.

"How do you get flowers to grow?"

The young manager replied, "That's simple, you plant some seeds."

"What must happen to those seeds in order for the flower to burst forth?"

"I don't know, the seeds get buried."

"That's right, as the seed is buried and dies the flower is born."

The young manager thought about this for several minutes.

Then Q said, "So, by burying it, it will bring growth in a completely new way!"

Q let the words hang in the air.

Then he said, "Change is one of the mysteries of life. That is why allowing it can be so exciting. A caterpillar must submit to a process that must feel like death in order to become a butterfly. A seed falls into the ground and dies; from it springs life. We must trust our Creator that life will follow death. Changes, when submitted to, will bring forth life. It is a unwritten rule of the universe that we see going on all around us.

"C. S. Lewis talked about this process of death and life going on all around us. He said: 'This principle holds in everyday matters. Even in social life, you will never make a good impression on other people until you stop thinking about what sort of impression you are making. (Die to what they think about you.) Even in literature and art, no man who focuses on originality will ever be original. Whereas if you simply try to tell the truth (without caring two pence how often it has been told before) you will, nine times out of 10, become original without ever having noticed it. This principle runs through all life from the top to bottom. Give up yourself, and you will find your real self. Lose your life and you will save it. Submit to death, death of your ambitions and favorite wishes every day and you will find life. Keep back nothing. Nothing that you have not given away will ever be really yours. Nothing in you that has not died will ever be raised from the dead. Look for yourself, and you will find in the long run only hatred, loneliness, despair, rage, ruin, and decay.'" [4]

"Wow, I never thought of it like that. I have to think about this some more," the young manager said, shaking his head.

Q smiled, "If we see change as the planting of seeds, of new growth, joys and pleasures yet to be discovered, a passage to get our wings, then it gives meaning to the pain of change."

The young manager left with thoughts full on new life and the cost of letting it come forth.

LEARNING INVOLVES:

Recognizing something's value.
The clearer the value of something, the easier the choice is. The greatest challenge for those involved in decision making is gaining clarity of value. Clarifying values is one of the key ingredients of learning.

Understanding that a choice is our way of investing ourselves in valuable things.
The choices we make represent our identity and what we value. The more you have chosen and have invested in something, the harder it will be to give it up.

Being aware that any change in where we invest ourselves, requires that a part of ourselves die.
Life grows when we lay part of ourselves down so that another part of ourselves may come to life. We need to see change as costly, yet as key for allowing room and providing fertilizer for new growth. A new beginning always begins with an ending.

Chapter Six

WHY CAN'T I SEE THE PROBLEM?

*The searcher's eye not seldom
finds more than he wished to find.*
Gotthold Ephraim Lessing 1779

People only see what they are prepared to see.
Emerson

*Two men look out through the bars: One sees the
mud, and one the stars.*
William Langland

*Perception is selective: A bald man sees non-bald
men as abnormally hairy.*

The young manager was trying to take the changes as slowly as possible. He could see different ones struggling with the changes as they met together. He could sense them holding on to that part of themselves, not wanting to let go. He realized they were probably focusing on the cost of the change, so he called them together to discuss it. The meeting lasted most of the afternoon as they discussed why the changes were needed. He found this really helped and everyone agreed on the changes except one person. He could not see how the changes could help and was dragging his feet. The young manager was getting frustrated, not knowing if he should move ahead or wait for him. He kept asking himself, "why can't he see the need for change?"

The young manager looked out the window and wished he could talk with his friend. He was confused and needed an outside voice. Tuesday came and he looked out the window but Q was not on the bench. An old person in a large trench coat, drooping hat and glasses had taken over their spot. He walked all the way around the walk-way and still didn't see Q. He wondered what Q could be trying to teach him now.

Another week passed and still no Q, the young manager finally grabbed his coat and went for a walk. The bench was empty so he sat down and tried to think.

A gentle movement of the bench signaled someone was sitting down. He looked over and saw the little old man with the large trench coat, drooping hat and glasses. He turned away and was just starting to get up when he heard the little old man ask, "Mind if I borrow a little bit of your bench for a while?"

The young manager stared in amazement.

The little old man straightened up, pulled his glasses off, and looked over at the young manager.

The young manager continued to stare.

"You fooled me!" he finally said.

Q smirked as he took off the large trench coat and drooping hat.

"I wanted to see if you were stuck in how you looked at things. Remember how we talked about our mental maps and how they influence what we see. You never bothered to try and find me this way."

The young manager sat back into the bench and laughed.

"I should have known."

Q grinned and finally said, "A few years ago, a school in England had a mix-up with a computer. Classes were put together with names of students sent out to teachers mentioning which students were supposed to be the smart ones and which the slow ones. A couple months went by, and the office people realized a horrible mistake had been made. The computer had mixed the labels on the students so that the smart students were labeled slow and the slow students were labeled smart."

The young manager said, "Somebody was going to catch it for that."

Q leaned over and whispered with a twinkle in his eye, "Never trust computers or IQ tests to tell you if you are smart, they don't know."

He sat back and continued, "Well some researchers looked into what happened in the classes with the teacher and students."

"Do you know what they found?"

"They were like that fish. They died from experience!" the young manager said trying not to laugh.

"No," Q grimaced, "they found out that the expectations of the teachers had helped to change the students. When a teacher expected a student to be smart, and the student didn't get an answer, the teachers expected it was their own fault. The teachers changed their approach to help students understand the answers. Teachers expected them to be able to perform and the students rose to the challenge. When any of the supposedly slower students didn't get an answer, the teachers expected that was normal and didn't try to help them. These students' scores went down."

"Really?"

"You can look the research up yourself. Others have, it's called the Pygmalion effect. Here let me help you with this idea. "Look around and find where the color red is found."

The young manager looked around him.

"Now close your eyes."

"Now, tell me where all the blue things are!"

The young manager was silent for a couple of minutes and then said, "I don't know. I think there is a blue car in the lot, but I wasn't looking for blue."

"Right," Q said, "You expected me to ask you where the red things were, so you focused on them to the exclusion of other colors. Whatever you are looking for will be the focus of your attention. Other areas will be blocked out."

"Wow, that's right," said the young manager.

"You had expectations of what I would look like, and when those were not met, you gave up. You did not think to take a risk and explore or examine your expectations before you made your decisions. "

The young manager sat shaking his head. "How could I have known it was you? You looked so different in that outfit!"

"The problem was I changed, and you didn't think of looking for me in a new way, to try and break from the picture you had developed of me! Expectations can be silent killers if we are not careful," commented Q.

"That is really tough to do!" said the young manager, frustrated.

Q allowed the young manager to stew before continuing, "You have lost the joy in investigating or exploring before you make a judgment. I have been sitting on our bench for a week now and you didn't even bother to get curious or explore a new thought. You saw me sitting here in this outfit and walked right past me without even thinking about it."

The young manager let out a deep breath. "I guess you are right."

Q frowned. "The important point is not who is right or wrong, but of learning. You must learn to explore your world because what you see can trick you. When you get stuck, a key is to step back and explore your perception to see why. When others get stuck, step into their world view and ask why. A simple rule is 'ask why at least five times', then, you will start to get to the root of the problem. When you are willing to investigate what you see and try to look from as many different ways as possible, you will then be able to find the things that are changing and the things that are not."

The young manager looked up for a few moments and then asked, "Is that why you said, 'perceived' value last time we met? What we see as valuable can change?"

Q nodded and said, "Our focus or perception is always limited. We are sometimes like a little boy who sees that a nickel is bigger than a dime and so thinks it is more valuable. He wants the nickel and you can't convince him that it is not more valuable than a dime. He outgrows that quick enough. Unfortunately, with some of our choices it is not so easy to outgrow them. We might choose some kind of relationship, lifestyle or fashion and then reality comes crashing in and we realize it was not what we valued it to be. When we realize we have spent part of our life on things of little value, we have these awakening moments that shake us up.

Q let these thoughts sink in for a second and then asked, "How is work going?"

The young manager thought about Q's disguise and how his own expectations and mental maps could blind him from seeing what is really going on.

"I thought I had some more questions for you, but I think they have already been answered. I am stuck in my thinking in the office, and I need to explore some 'why's' before I make judgments about what is really wrong."

Q smiled and said, "I will leave you with a thought from Einstein: 'You can't fix a problem with the same mind set that created it.'"

So the young manager went back to work determined to try and see his problems in new ways. Maybe they weren't problems, just opportunities hidden from his sight.

Little did he know that new challenges were just on the horizon that would push him far beyond what he thought he could do.

LEARNING DISCERNS:

<u>What you see grows out of the "map" in your mind</u>.

      Your mind is the interpreter of the language of sight. It tells you the meaning of the things you see. Your perspective is called your point of view or a paradigm. It is not "reality," it is your interpretation of reality.

<u>What you expect to see, you will see, what you are looking for, you will find</u>.

      Expectations are like a "sight" on a gun. They narrow the field of vision down to a very specific area. The things you have learned in the past tempt you to narrowly focus your perspective. Take the "sight" off every once in a while and look around to see where you are and what is happening.

<u>There is a joy in exploration that you will never find when you are limited to "your" field of vision</u>.

      Discipline yourself to get in your staff and customers' shoes and see what they see. What do they feel? What do they hear? What do they smell or taste?

FAMOUS MISPERCEPTIONS

"The South has too much common sense and good temper to break up the Union." Abraham Lincoln, 1860.

"That's an amazing invention, but who would ever want to use one of them." Rutherford B. Hayes in 1876 after witnessing a demonstration of the telephone.

"The phonograph is of no commercial value." Thomas Edison, 1880.

"Believe me, Germany is unable to wage war." David Lloyd George, former Prime Minister of Great Britain, 1934.

"'Gone with the Wind' is going to be the biggest flop in Hollywood history. I'm just glad it'll be Clark Gable who's falling flat on his face and not Gary Cooper." Gary Cooper, 1938.

"I think there is a world market for about five computers." Thomas J. Watson, Chairman of Board of IBM, 1943.

Chapter Seven

HOW MUCH DO I KNOW?

*It is the memory that enables a person
to gather roses in January.*

*Advice is like snow; the softer it falls,
the longer it dwells upon,
and the deeper it sinks into, the mind.
Samuel Taylor Coleridge*

*To profit from good advice requires as much
wisdom as to give it.*

The young manager welcomed the staff person into his office and asked him to please have a seat. "I don't think I have heard you clearly. You are concerned about the changes we have been talking about and I want to hear what you see as potential problems. I realize I have not been willing to see things from your point of view and I need you to help me understand where you see the problems in this change."

The staff person hesitated and then started to talk. An hour slid past and the young manager thanked the staff person again for his thoughts and said good bye. He marveled at how helpful the comments were and how fruitful the time had been. He just couldn't say what he needed to in a group setting. That was what was blocking him from working through the changes. Fixing the problem seemed so simple, yet he would have never found out if he had not sat down personally with the man and asked him his point of view.

He just had time to get to the meeting with the Vice President of finances. He nervously walked into his office and was greeted.

"Sit down son,"

The young manager sat down and the Vice President began.

"You know I am not one to beat around the bush so let me lay out what I think. I believe that how things have been done before is more important than thinking about how they will be done in future. I don't trust anything that wasn't invented here. I believe how we did things under the grand old boss is the only way they should be done. I don't believe sitting around contemplating your navel does any good. I like action, and I think the best worker is seen and not heard. That may be old school, but it works. You hear me?"

The young manager nodded his head and said, "Yes sir."

"Good," continued the Vice President, "Now, down to business. Since our last meeting you have done very well. I need a new regional manager and some of the other vice presidents think you should join the team. Personally, I think you are too young and too new here, but we are going to give you a chance. Let me emphasize the word 'chance'."

The young manager walked out the door into the air and felt much better. The walls were starting to close in on him again. He was excited on the one hand and terrified on the other. What if he couldn't make it work? He had already put his family under a lot of pressure. He just didn't have any more energy to throw at this new position. The added responsibility could push him over the edge, but the extra money would be nice to help clear up the bills. Maybe even put braces on his little girl.

He needed to find his teacher and talk. The bench was empty so he continued on. He walked past another bench and still no sign of his teacher. He continued around the walkway, slowed his pace, and began to look around to explore his surroundings. Just ahead he saw Q and breathed a sigh of relief. He recognized him without any problem.

Q smiled when he saw his student and said to him when they met, "We are really exploring new ground. You have come a long way to find me."

The young manager smiled.

"I have good news and bad news."

Q had a look of concern on his face.

"The bad news first please. Are you being asked to move?"

The young manager took a deep breath and looked around.

"I have been asked to take over the region. I just talked with the vice president of finance and even though I only recently moved into this place, my boss is being transferred and he has put in my name to take his place."

Q reached out to shake his hand and said, "Congratulations, I am thrilled. You'll do a great job."

"Thank you. That is good news, but honestly, it's also bad news. I don't know if I can take the added pressure. I only know my area of expertise and now I have to manage more people, and they have different areas of expertise."

Q nodded his head and said, "My brother told me that when he had reached the role of executive director, 'The crazy thing is that you work for a top position throughout your career. You become more and more specialized and more and more valued. Then you are finally promoted to the board, get your title and all the perks, only to find that it's a hollow joke. You are suddenly expected to be omniscient. You are meant to know everything about everything. The truth is that you know a lot about very little because you have become so specialized. Yet there seems to be no way of saying 'help!' so people at the top often feel uncomfortable, resentful, and cannot do what they are paid to do.' Does that sound familiar?"

"Yes, very, but maybe my new position is still specialized enough to keep me in a place where I feel a little comfortable," responded the young manager.

The teacher started walking and the young manager fell in step with him.

"Tell me what you have learned so far."

The young manager thought back over all that had been going on.

"Well, let me see. I have learned that what I see is not always enough. I need to explore so that I get as much information as I can before I make a decision. I will always have a limited view, and that is why I need others to help me see things as clearly as possible."

"Good," Q said.

Encouraged, he continued, "I have learned that my education doesn't automatically make me a learner and not knowing an answer does not make me incompetent. It's okay not to know as it is an opportunity to grow and learn about new things. Asking questions is good and does not show that I am stupid."

"Well said!" chimed the teacher.

"I have also learned that there are different kinds of change going on all around us. Because everything that's alive is changing, I need to keep my eyes open to this."

"Everything is changing, including you," commented the teacher.

"I have also learned there are maps in my mind. That my mind is constantly rewiring itself as it interacts with what I think, see, hear or experience and that my mind creates maps or patterns to help keep it all organized. These mental maps are models that provide security as I can remember what I have learned from the past. This also helps in working with others. I can expect them to act the way they normally do. These maps or traditions are important and are expressions of values."

"Brain maps create traditions that provide security for us. Good!"

"I have learned that all of us have a natural desire for risk or growth as you can't grow without a risk. This tension keeps us from getting stuck in traditions or cultures that don't fit anymore. Risk is scary and really hard because we become vulnerable and that makes it easier for others to trip us or knock us down."

The young manager looked over at the teacher at this point and glared at him as if he was somehow hurt.

"You remember, good!" the teacher laughed.

"I have learned that one of the hardest things about change is that when you change, you must be willing to let a part of yourself, that it's often through death that new growth comes forth. To find new opportunities we must be willing to die to old things and the part of me that is attached to them."

They had walked all the way back to the first green bench and sat down.

They both sat quietly as they thought about all that had been said.

Q broke the silence.

"You know these ideas in your head. Now's the time for you to test them as you work with the new team. We have come back to where we started on this green bench."

Q smiled and added, "You remind me of a student who came to me at the end of the school year. She looked up at me and with big tears in her eyes, and said, 'I don't want to go to another class next year. I want to stay in this class with you.'"

Q looked over at the young manager and said, "I tried to convince my little friend that my job was to prepare her for the next grade. That she needed to step out and learn new things. In the end she agreed she would if she could come and visit me anytime she felt scared. I agreed.

"I would like to stick around and watch the fun but first, I am going to be gone for three weeks to help in some orphanages in China. I will be back soon enough. I suppose you may have a few more questions for me as you try to put what you have learned to practice."

"Three weeks huh," the young manager said slowly. "I guess that will give me time to work on these things. Have a great trip and I will see you when you get back."

So the young manager went back to work, amazed at all he had learned in such a short time, and thinking about how he could apply them to his new job.

LEARNING:

Gives us freedom not to know, and joy in the process of finding out.

Sees change as normal to a healthy life.

Creates unique maps in our mind.

Knows there is no growth without risk.

Involves being aware that when we change our choice of how we invest ourselves, part of us dies with the change.

Knows our view is incomplete and works hard to fill in the missing pieces by asking for others point of view.

SECTION
II

Chapter Eight

CAN'T I JUST TELL PEOPLE
WHAT TO LEARN?

*To know the pains of power, we must go to those
who have it; to know its pleasures, we must go to
those who are seeking it.*
Charles Caleb Coltan

Weeks went by and the young manager was promoted to regional director. He was excited about the promotion and he knew what he wanted to accomplish. He thought out his plan in exacting details. He called the managers together and put it all out on the table. He then met with each of the different managers below him and wanted complete details of their schedules, people and specific jobs. At first he felt like he was getting his message across, but after six or seven individual meetings he could feel the rising tension from them. With the tension he became nervous and tried to figure out how he could get them to do what he wanted. He tried asking for more reports. As more and more details swept in, it felt like an information typhoon gathering momentum. Everything was getting mixed up.

He decided to go for a walk to try and catch his breath. He hoped maybe Q was around. He headed toward the green bench.

As the young manager sat and quietly reflected on his challenge to get his plan accomplished, a mother strolled past with her young child. The little boy, full of energy, darted off for the grass but was stopped in his footsteps. The young manager looked closer and realized the youngster wore a harness and from the back of the harness a leash. The young manager corrected himself. Dogs have leashes, young children have... he couldn't think of the right word. A rope? Whatever it was called, it ended up firmly in the mother's hand. She had control. What an interesting idea he thought, protect your child and make life much easier for yourself. He let his mind wander and pictured his managers sitting around the table all tied to a leash ending firmly in his hand. A picture of his twelve year old son with a harness and rope leading to his hand jumped into his mind. He shook his head. It wouldn't work. He began to think about the managers below him and how he was trying to work through them.

Q walked over and sat down. "Well, how is the new regional director?"

"Good. Challenged, but good," responded the young manager. "How was your trip?"

Thinking for a second, Q responded, "It was great. I love being around children and there is so much to do. Runny noses, muddy faces, scraped knees, little bodies exploding with energy. I was running around helping mouths find food, stopping missiles launched by little hands, and touching their little hearts because I care. I can't speak much Chinese but we can touch hearts. I must admit it's painful to see the children in those poor conditions. I want to go back and help more when I can. You want to take a trip with me one day?"

"Uh, I never thought about it but I am sure it would be an adventure."

"Great, then we can take a trip after things settle down for you. I would love to have company on a trip and it might open your eyes to seeing things in new ways," Q responded.

The young manager said as he pointed at the mother walking with her son, "I saw that mother walking by with her son and I began thinking about my job and trying to accomplish my plans."

"I saw the mother," Q agreed.

The young manager continued, "I see some analogies between the mother and my leadership over the managers. I guess I have been like that mother. I would like to control my manager's experiences and show them exactly what I think they need and what they are ready for. I have been trying to gather and watch over every detail of their schedules and through that to keep each one on a tight leash. That's not how it works, is it?"

Q sat quietly, watching the wind pushing its way around. The trees resisted with only their leaves whispering and teasing the wind to try harder. The bushes held each other tightly and only gave in a little, the tall grass flowed, bobbing up and down in enjoyment.

The young manager asked, "I know power, control and learning are connected, but I can't get the relationship between them straight in my head. How does power or control affect learning?"

"That is the million dollar question!" Q responded. "Years ago, I realized this was the question I faced as a teacher. I believe it is the major question all teachers and managers must face. It is, at heart, a question about learning."

The young manager thought out loud, "I can see that learning is about taking risks, changing, and new growth. I can also see that the negative side of control or maybe I should say, power, is about avoiding risks. I think I have some really good ideas about what to do, but I know I can't force them on those below me. Also, I guess I hate to admit it but in looking over the first couple of weeks as a regional director, I was afraid to fail or that those below me would fail and I used my power to protect myself. I tried to make sure I knew everything that everyone was doing and to establish my control. I kept the other managers on the organizational leash so I wouldn't feel vulnerable. It is one thing to take a risk among a few fellow staff members; it is another to be the leader among leaders and take a risk."

"So much to learn in such a short amount of time. What a great learning opportunity," remarked Q .

"Haven't I already blown it? You said the first time you do something is key!"

"Well, let's say you may not have started off on the right foot but there is no time like the present to learn and change. First you can learn that failure can be an intimate teacher. Success doesn't always teach you things. Many times you don't know why it worked. Success may only ask you to copy it, ad infinitum. Failure is a master teacher few will willingly embrace. We don't need to fear failure, we should only fear *not* learning from failure. That is a true failure, to not learn from experience is a great loss.

"On the average, it is estimated that a successful entrepreneur fails nine times for every successful venture. The great scientist and inventor, Thomas Edison, when he was trying to find the filament for the light bulb, had tried over a thousand different elements. When someone asked him how he could continue on after so many failures he said, 'I haven't failed. I have learned what will not work.' Giving people freedom to learn is giving them freedom to fail, and that includes giving yourself freedom to fail and learn."

The young manager slowly nodded and said, "That's why there is always a risk in allowing others and myself to learn. Chances are, it may cost me in the process."

"That's right," Q said. "I've heard of a great example that shows how another manager dealt with failure and learning. This manager, after hearing that one of his staff made some bad decisions costing the company millions of dollars, called him into the office."

The manager listened to the young man's story.

Silence hung in the room as the old manager waited. Finally the young man asked, 'Am I fired, sir?'

"The manager laughed and said, 'Are you kidding? We just gave you a million dollar education; we can't afford to let you go. Just don't let it happen again.' The young manager left having learned a valuable - and expensive - lesson. He knew he could do better - and he did."

Q asked the young manager a question. "So how do you create a learning team without using power?"

The young manager leaned back and finally said, "That's a hard question; I'm not sure. Since the team should be constantly changing, adapting, and responding to their world, they must be able to adjust on their own. But on the other hand, if I can't know and dictate all the actions of a team, how can I manage? It would seem like I would just have chaos."

Q said, "My friend told me the other day of a basic mental pattern or assumption he was having to break in his thinking. It was, 'The level of incompetence is always one level below you.'[5] I think we all struggle with that. When we think of those below us as incompetent, we are tempted to use our power to protect us from their failures. When they feel dominated, they feel they don't have a choice and therefore, they often give up their sense of responsibility or ownership. We perceive this as proof of our assumption that they are incompetent and take on more and more of their responsibilities, until it stops us from being effective."

"Here," Q said as he took a pencil and a scrap of paper out of his pocket and drew a rectangle. "This simple diagram will show you the tension between form and freedom."

Form   Freedom

"I will use *form* instead of control as control is a hard word to use clearly since it means so many different things. It may mean manage, direct, subdue, discipline, steer, conquer or restrain. We all want and need *forms* of control but it really depends on the context and paradigm or attitude it grows out of."

Q pointed at the diagram and said, "On this side is *form*. It is the structure, hierarchy, span of control, etc. and can be seen, as an extreme, in a military model. Although I have heard they are changing, they have rules and regulations, treated like a bible, that says how everything should be done. The military doesn't handle change at all if there isn't a set procedure for dealing with it. Like a machine, you have a standard input, an exact process where each part plays the same role over and over again, and you have the same output every time."

The young manager looked at the line cutting across and said, "So if you have a lot of form, you will have little freedom to learn, and change will be very difficult."

"That's right," Q said. "In many business areas, we have moved past the industrial era into the information era. Businesses in our day require lightening fast changes, flexibility, on your feet thinking, quick starting and the full involvement of everyone. With this pressure pushing all businesses, they must look at the form they use so as to promote the highest freedom possible in any situation. I read the other day that the average lifetime of the largest industrial enterprises is probably less than half the average lifetime of a person in an industrialized society. [6] In fact, one-third of the Fortune 500 industrial organizations listed in 1970 ceased to exist by 1983. Unless companies learn to adapt they cannot survive long in our time."

The young manager asked, "Would change have the same challenges for organizations as it does for people? I mean, we talked about patterns in our mind setting up how we do things, but organizations don't have 'minds' to create patterns, do they?"

"They do have a collective 'mind'," Q answered. "Organizations *form* patterns for how to get things done to save its collective energy. There is also a kind of death that goes on when an organization changes its *form*. Did you ever wonder why, once an organization is created no one wants to 'kill' it. Think of the government programs that have far out lived their purpose but no one wants to be responsible to bury it."

"I never thought about that, but it's right. What about the other side, what do you mean by freedom? Everybody doing their own thing?" the young manager asked.

"No. If everybody wanted to do their own thing, that is when you need a strong form to force them all together. Freedom on the other side is about ownership. They will provide the self-control, *form*, needed to accomplish the tasks. Moving from external control to allowing learning in freedom is a challenge every leader must walk through." Q chuckled and continued on, " I can remember the first day I walked into class as a student teacher. I had all these ideas about how to do things and I was going to show the others that I had it all together. "

Q shook his head, "I didn't know it, but I had a lot to learn. Thankfully, we had a teacher at my first school who was so smooth. Kids would fight to get in her class. She had taught for 30 years. And I don't mean one year duplicated 30 times. Each year was different depending on the class. You could always hear laughter coming from her room and the kids respected her.

During that first year she helped me a lot. I remember one time, I was trying to teach my second graders what commas, periods and exclamation marks meant. After several explanations focusing on the fact that commas meant slow down, periods meant stop or pause, and exclamation marks meant emphasis -- I figured they should know punctuation with no problem. I then had them read aloud. They were not getting it.

"I tried again and again in vain. I started to get upset, and I was going to make them understand. They were my students, and they were going to learn even if they had to stay in during recess!"

"This teacher heard me having problems and jumped in to help me. She had them follow her outside. She told them, 'I am going to read to you and I want you to walk around in a circle. When I say 'comma' I want you to slow down, whenever I say 'period' I want you to stop dead in your tracks, and when I say 'exclamation mark' I want you to jump up and down. The kids mingled around smiling and jumping to make sure their 'jumper' was working. She tried this for five minutes with complete success. She then gave me back my class and asked me to take them back inside and try reading aloud with them. When they went back inside and read, all of them slowed down at the commas, paused at periods, and used emphasis at exclamation points."

Q smiled as he remembered her help.

"I learned a very important principle that day that I have never forgotten. Everyone wants to learn, they just need information put to them in the right way. The form was wrong for them. I thought I could make those kids learn. My turning to power was not rooted in strength but in my own weakness."

They were both silent for a minute as they thought about the words. The wind continued its assault around them as they sat and pondered.

"A few years later, I had broken up a class of older kids into learning teams and appointed one of the girls a leader of a team. She came up to me at the end of class frustrated, not knowing what to do with her team. As school was over for the day, I went on a walk with her and we began talking about it. She was wanting to tell everyone what to do and how to do it. I had her jump on her bike and ride around for a second. I asked if that was how she wanted to run the team. They were like the bike to her, under her control to steer, to speed up or slow down, adjusted to her comfort and style and without any say in the process. She smiled. 'That would be great.'"

Q stopped for a second and then said to the young manager, "It was her project; they were an extension of her in her mind."

He continued on, "I asked this little leader, 'How do they feel when they understand all you want to do is use them?' she thought for a second and said, 'I guess that is why we have had some problems.' I told her, 'Don't think of them like a machine at your disposal, but think more of them like a basketball team or a high wire act where you each need each other in order to be effective."

"Did she learn that?"

"It took her half the year, but in the end her group was the most effective group. When we use our power, trying to focus on me or my way, what I want done, those below us sense it and stop growing and lose any sense of ownership. Remember we used the word order? You can still have order but you must be willing to change how you work with people. You have to be willing to share power with them. The word managers use is 'empowering' people."

The young manager thought for a moment and then said, "Well, if a young student can learn, then I must be able to."

"We are all students when it comes to learning," Q said. "Understanding the *form* needed with each person, team and process is key. Machines don't learn, people do. You must teach those around you the variety of the different structures or *forms* needed so that at one time they can carefully control a manufacturing process so that there is no error and at other times allow challenges to the hidden assumptions of what is being done so that it could be improved.

"The order or orchestration we all want cannot be found through dominating control or extending 'my' power. When we manage that way it kills human freedom by eliminating choice and ultimately, it destroys learning, bringing people down to the level of machinery."

The young manager jumped in with a sly grin, "Everywhere I have ever worked has been run this way. Machines are easier to control."

Q nodded his head with understanding and said, "When you work with people, you become an orchestrator, weaving things together in patterns that have yet to be seen by any other group. As each group is different, how you work together and what you produce will be different."

The young manager thought for a second and then said, "I only want to ask one thing, how do I do this?"

Q leaned forward and whispered, "You already know several ways, the first question for you is are you personally willing to take a risk?

"If you've not made the choice that you are willing to step out, take a risk and orchestrate rather than dominate, what you do won't matter. As you know, leadership is an art that requires hard work to learn. For those under you, trust can only emerge when you let go of dominating control."

The young manager stared at the world hurrying past him, people walking by, leaves blown by the wind, birds hovering. A part of him was inspired and wanted to step out, another wanted to run for cover and not listen.

"I was afraid you would say that. What did you say the other day about dying and risk? I guess this is a chance to trust that life comes when I am willing to let my reputation go."

He chuckled and remarked, "What a strange world we live in."

"I can't argue with that," responded the teacher. "Remember, just because you're not in complete control, doesn't mean everything is out of control. [7] Think about this, and let's meet again next week."

LEARNING DISCOVERS:

Dominating control or power is the weak manager's way of avoiding vulnerability and risk.

Control can be good and needed at times. In emergency situations when we don't have time to learn, those with authority, experience and wisdom need to take control. Long term survival doesn't depend on control, it depends on learning.

Form varies for each group and season.

Freedom is the goal. A manager wants to move his team to ownership as quickly as possible as this offers the best chances for learning. The only way to survive in the long term is by learning.

You can't force anyone to learn anything of value.

Almost everyone wants to learn, they just need to hear it, see it or experience it in a way they can understand.

Order is good. It gives boundaries and agrees on expectations.

The wise manager orchestrates his team using each person in the place they fit best.

Predictability through control is not good. It puts humans on a level with machines. Machines don't learn very well.

"We must give up our trust in stability in trying to predetermine where we will be in five years, and trust our ability to learn and discover where we should go."

"The control we talked about is a wrong way of getting what we really want. What we really want is order with freedom. Order is the sense or understanding that there are boundaries, that each person has a part to play and yet in the midst of it all, is this risk, because you don't know exactly what is going to happen next, and you sense the vulnerability and challenge of it.

Where the supervisor relied on controls to coordinate and focus work activity, the team leader now relies on information instead.
Kimball Fisher 7

Chapter Nine

HOW DO I HELP THEM LEARN?

Everything that is really great and inspiring is created by the individual who can labor in freedom.
Einstein

It's a vice to trust all, and equally a vice to trust none.
Seneca

The next week the wise old teacher and the inquisitive young student sat on the green bench watching enormous dark clouds challenging each other's supremacy as they raced across the sky.

"Did you figure out whether you were going to take a risk?"

"I did. I met with each of the different area managers and began to assess what they needed from me and what I needed from them. I began to look at what would be the best form for each one and then looked at what steps they could make towards freedom. I guess I took them by surprise as it was a change from the way I had been dealing with them. It may take a little time for them to see I mean it."

"Good job," Q replied warmly. "The best way to show you mean it is by focusing your energy on the environment they work in. People can pull energy from their environment to strengthen themselves or they will spend energy protecting themselves. The type of environment people find themselves in will influence their learning, growth and their ability to manage change."

The young manager responded, "Yeah, I can see that."

"Good." said Q. "Each person under you is different. If you want people to learn on a daily basis how to be more effective and to spend their energy working with you, not against your control, you must create a climate that accepts, allows and respects uncertainty.

You must provide a safe place in which to work and learn."

Q leaned back on the bench and continued, "This reminds me of a study on children playing in a school playground with no fence versus children playing in a school playground surrounded by chain link fence. Do you know what the researchers found?"

"I don't have a clue."

"They found that on the playground with no fence, kids tended to play in the middle as protective boundaries were not clear and they felt unsafe. The kids on the playground with a fence played all over the playground right out to the fence. The protective boundaries were very clear and they felt safe.

"We need clear protected boundaries and security if we are to grow and use all that we have."

Q watched a father walk by holding his child's hand then continued, "The funny thing about learning and growth is that it is frequently preceded by periods of uncertainty, ambiguity or imbalance. As this all takes place, we need a safe place or we will cut short the learning process."

The young manager smiled and said, "I must be learning a lot because there is uncertainty, ambiguity and imbalance all around me."

Q smiled, pointed to his head and said, "I am talking about up here."

The young manager responded, "There is a lot up there too."

"Good." Q replied smiling. "Karl Pribram calls this aspect of learning 'active uncertainty.' He goes on to say how absolutely critical active uncertainty is to helping the brain make maximum connections and that learning can proceed smoothly only in an atmosphere of general safety and sufficient challenge.[8]"

The young manager thought for a minute and then said, "So if I provide a safe environment where people can make mistakes and feel secure, then they will be much more open to change, growth and learning"

"That's right," Q said and continued, "One thing they never taught me in school and I doubt they ever teach managers, is that leading, be it through teaching or managing, often proceeds through guess work. Like a painter, you must discern whether further brush strokes will weaken rather than strengthen your work."

"The true function of a leader is to create the most favorable conditions for ongoing effectiveness, of which learning and growth is a key part. Form is important as it also protects those who are involved. Remember, people want to grow and learn. They want to be effective and competent. A major dimension of this artistry involves seizing the moment, when you see there are things they can learn."

Q leaned back, and smiled, "I remember an elderly teacher once brought a student to me holding him by the ear. The poor little guy was standing on his toes trying not to have his ear pulled off. She held him there before me like a prize and said indignantly, 'You know the new cement we are pouring by the cafeteria? I caught this young man writing his name in it.' She then let go of his ear and his heels plopped to the ground. I told her I would take care of the matter."

Q grew quiet as he thought back to that day.

"Well, what did you do?" asked the young manager.

With a huge smile Q replied, "I congratulated him."

The young manager wrinkled his forehead and leaned forward, "You what?"

"It was a window of opportunity to teach him a much bigger lesson. I told the boy that I was impressed that he wanted to have his name remembered. That is a wonderful goal and I encouraged him to not lose that desire to make an impact on the world."

The young manager shook his head.

"I also told him that the cement by the cafeteria wasn't a very good place to leave his name, that maybe we should go and tell the work man and see if we could make it right."

Q paused and looked over at the young manager and continued, "He was ready to learn. He needed to understand that it was a perfectly natural desire to want your name in a permanent place and that it should to be focused rather than pinched or squashed away. Besides, the teacher had caused him enough pain."

The young manager pondered this and said, "So if uncertainty or guess work is so important, I will never have blueprints that show me exactly what to do!"

Q replied, "It goes back to the start, about it being okay not to know all the answers. I assure you that this idea is not new. This truth has been around for several thousand years. In 'The Art of War', [9] Sunzi says this about military leaders going to battle." Q leaned over and whispered, "This is a loose translation but you will get the idea. Sunzi said, 'The principle of deploying forces is that there are no certain methods. Just like flowing water, which is constantly changing direction. So there are not certain rules for deployment -- just use your strengths and protect your weaknesses. Alternate your tactics according to the circumstances.'"

Silence hung in the air.

Finally Q spoke. "No one can know, absolutely, what is the next best thing to do. We might as well acknowledge this and work with the potential insecurity rather than against it. When a leader takes risks and creates an atmosphere of stability and familiarity, then people will be much more willing to step out and take risks in their own areas of expertise and interests.

"However, when people are under somebody's thumb, where there is tight control and everyone's job's at risk, when competition is promoted, an atmosphere of fear and stress is created. This shuts down learning, which cuts off exploration and creativity. And finally, we go right into a defensive pattern of thinking."

Q stopped for a second as a pigeon landed close by and then went on, "We have a name for this phenomenon in education. A researcher named Leslie Hart calls this "downshifting."[10] Downshifting is roughly like a camera lens that has a reduced focus. This narrowing and slowing occurs when an individual perceives an experience as threatening. When we downshift, we revert to the tried and true traditions and follow old beliefs and behaviors, regardless of what opportunities are available. Our responses become more automatic and limited. We are less able to access all that we know or see what is really "there." With the speed that life is changing all around us, if you can't be on the cutting edge of seeing opportunities and taking risks, your business is soon left in the dust."

The young manager turned to Q, "So, how can I challenge them in their work and at the same time have a safe environment? I can imagine all my people floating around the office safe and secure but not getting the job done. My boss wants proof that we are doing something. How do I do that?"

"Good point. I am not saying there should be no challenge, it's threat you have to watch out for. They have a very different meaning. Threat is directly linked to helplessness. We are back to power again, when people have no choice and things are beyond their control, they feel helpless. Challenge is seeing their abilities used to accomplish an objective that stirs them to reach beyond themselves. Your staff will downshift under perceived threat and will learn optimally when appropriately challenged."

Q took a deep breath and continued, "We talked about this earlier. There is no growth, there is no development, there is no learning without risk or tension. Tension is absolutely indispensable to the process. This tension is the challenge for people to be more than they can be, and to allow them to take risks as they step out to go beyond themselves. Do you remember us talking about this challenge?" Q asked.

"Is this the balance... No, wait a second," the young manager said holding up his hand.

"Balance is not the word we used. Tension. It is the tension between tradition and risk. Remembering what we have learned from our past and taking new steps to be creative in the situation we find ourselves in. Isn't this just another way of talking about the struggle between form and freedom?" the young manager asked.

"That's right," Q answered beaming from ear to ear. "The form is the cultures and traditions and the freedom is the risk involved for individuals to be unique. There's a popular teacher named Stephen Covey, who said, 'Many truly great classes or, in your case, your office, teeter on the very edge of chaos. Synergy tests whether managers and the team are really open to the principle of the whole being greater than the sum of its parts. Many times neither the manager nor his team knows for sure what is going to happen."[11]

The teacher paused for a second and then continued, "You see, everyone knows he or she can play a part. This desire is woven within the fabric of each being. Risk stirs each person to do more than they are doing now. Each of your staff wants to understand they are playing a significant part which is challenging and meaningful. They sense they have a destiny and are looking to find it."

Q stopped and pointed at a young child, hands extended, barely able to reach the handle on its own carriage, pushing with all his might. His mother walking down the path alongside him, offering help when he needed it. "Even children long to play a part in their world."

The young manager watched the young struggling child and his mother walk past and then said, "I see. My job is to provide a challenge that allows people to see how they can get involved in solving or accomplishing meaningful tasks. I am to cut off anything that communicates to them that they are helpless and just a part of the system."

"That's right, although it is not as simple as it sounds," said Q.

So the young manager went back to his office wanting to make it a place where people felt safe from threat and were challenged to step out and reach for more.

LEARNING PERCEIVES:

<u>Like a guest who can tell when it is wanted, and when it is not</u>.
It can see through talk easily. Actions speak louder than words. When a manager models learning by his life, his staff will follow the model.

<u>In order to spend the energy to learn, it must first be uncertain of what it knows.</u>
Old meanings must be given up. To allow uncertainty is to become vulnerable. We need safety to give up what we know to learn new things.

<u>Guess work may sometimes play a part when figuring out what to do next</u>.
No one wants to guess if their job on the line.

<u>Challenge is important</u>.
Challenges help us to take a risk. They push us to reach beyond ourselves and to, in a sense, find more of ourselves in the opportunity.

Chapter Ten

WHAT WILL MOTIVATE THEM TO LEARN?

*The most important and desirable things in the
human experience have no physical existence. One
of these is "meaning."*
Daniel Taylor

*"Meaning" is the most stirring of all
spiritual impulses...*
-Helmut Thielicke

*A rock pile ceases to be a rock pile the moment a
single man contemplates it, bearing within him
the image of a cathedral.*
Saint-Exupery

*No man sees far; the most see no further
than their noses.*
Count Cagliostro

*Man's search for meaning is the primary
motivation in his life...*
Victor Frankl

The young manager had been working hard to create a form that would protect those under him, giving them a sense of safety. He also met with them individually to work out some challenges. He called all the group together and wanted to get a sense from them about the important questions that they needed answers to. With a little help, soon the questions began to roll out.

"How can sales keep up when they don't even know what research is doing? What was the budget cut for? Why did the main office send over a new guy to check on follow up and service? Who..."

They were valid questions. Yet, it seemed the questions pulled them in different directions and he didn't know how to tie them all together. Each of them was only interested in their own area. He thanked them for their input and assured them he would get some answers. He knew where he would start. He headed off to the green bench to get some help.

"Research has questions, sales has questions, marketing has questions, personnel has questions. They are good questions and I know I need to draw them altogether but I don't know how without forcing myself on them. Any ideas?" The young manager asked.

Q pulled out a piece of notebook paper and said, "I am going to draw a picture, and I want you to draw a part of it."

He folded the piece of paper in half and then tore out a square piece from the middle of the folded paper, "Here, this is your piece," he said as he handed the young manager the small piece of paper.

The young manager unfolded the little piece of paper and stared.

"What are you going to draw?" he asked looking over at the blank piece of paper held by the teacher.

"I'm not sure yet of the details, but it will be a new house that I have been looking at and thinking about buying."

"What kind of house is it?" asked the young manager.

"Just a typical one story, two car garage house," replied Q.

"Where are you going to draw it on the paper? How many windows does the house have, and where are they? I can't draw my picture until you show me what you are going to do! Why don't you draw the house and then I will fit my piece in there after I see what you have done!"

It was now clear the young manager was frustrated at being asked to do something when he didn't know how his part fit in.

Q looked over at him with a smile, his eyes dancing.

"Tch, Tch, Tch, so impatient. You have so many questions!" He gently chided the young manager.

He then smiled and said, "Gotcha!"

The young manager leaned forward and put his head in his hands.

"When you call the managers into a meeting and ask them to fulfill certain expectations or job responsibilities, how clearly do they know what is expected of them? Do they see the big picture clearly? Do they know, that what they are doing is tied into that picture? How hard have you worked at getting the big picture from your boss so you can pass it on to those under you?"

"I hear you, they can't see the big picture so they were just acting like me," the young manager said as he looked at Q.

He continued, "This is what they were trying to teach me in school! We spent weeks studying all these abstract views of 'Vision' and its meaning, place and importance in leading and I see its purpose more clearly now than I ever did then."

Q could see he understood. He let the ideas sink in and then added, "Learning and meaning always starts with the context or the big picture as a frame of reference for the parts we are working on. The missing link is that people can't see how what they are doing has meaning and fits. Meaning is one of the vital pieces for motivating people and providing an opportunity for ownership. A key way to help them get that motivation is for them to see how their piece fits into the big picture and then their job will make sense. Finding meaning arouses energy. On a personal level it will make a much easier job in clarifying expectations and job descriptions."

Q grinned and said, "One time I drew a picture on a large piece of drawing paper and then cut it into smaller pieces. When the kids came into class I gave each one of them a piece of this puzzle and asked them what the big picture might look like. They shared some of the craziest ideas and then began asking questions."

Q leaned back and continued, "One little girl came up to me with tears in her eyes and said, 'My piece is almost blank.' I smiled at her and said 'Oh, but that is a very important piece.

"I put on the overhead a copy of the picture I had drawn so they could all see it. I then gave them the task of putting all the pieces together."

Q leaned over and said, "You should have seen their face when they realized they all had a piece. Each was different and they all had a part to play. The little girl tried to hide her piece and then she got excited when she realized her piece was needed, it had an important place, right in the middle, in helping them all fit together. I had never seen them work together like they did that day knowing that each had something to give. It was great!"

The young manager sat and thought of the people in his office. He wondered how clearly the managers owned and saw the big picture and if they believed their part had meaning to make the whole fit and work together.

He could see he had some business to do in the weeks ahead.

An idea came and he asked, "How does this tie into perception? Both have to do with how you see things."

Q pulled his head back with eyes wide open in mock surprise.

"We are thinking now." he said grinning. "Remember, perception is a matter of focus. When you are focusing your attention on one thing, you ignore other areas. When looking for red, you automatically lose most of the other colors."

The young manager shook his head and said, "Okay, I can see that."

Q continued, "When you remove threat from people's job, that changes their focus and allows them to see things in new or different ways. When people are scared, they focus on their own security and cut off everything else.

"When you give them the big picture, this gives them a reference point. They will all see it a little differently, but that is good. Their perception will help shape it into a clearer picture and bring ownership."

Q sat quietly and enjoyed watching his student think about what he was learning and how to apply it.

The young manager grinned. "So everyone has a piece they are focused on. The big picture is what I can do that gives them the context for what they are working on."

"That's right." Q said.

A few moments passed by as they each focused on their thoughts.

Finally Q handed the piece of paper with a hole in it to the young manager and said, "Put this up on your wall. It will remind you of what a key part of your work is all about. Remember, when the big picture is clear and has meaning to your staff as they see their piece fitting, they will identify with the big picture and begin to take ownership. Vision is a way of bringing meaning, not just a tool for seeing."

The young manager went to work with a new understanding of how important it was to see the big picture.

LEARNING KNOWS:

It starts with the big picture.
　　This gives all the smaller pieces a context. Each person will draw meaning for their work as they see how it fits in the big picture.

Each person will know how to work better with others, when he or she knows what part others are playing and how their job relates to the big picture.

Finding meaning motivates people to learn and brings fulfillment to the job.
　　'Vision' is not just about seeing the big picture. What they see must have meaning to them or it is only somebody else's picture. Ownership comes when they find their work having meaning in the big picture.

Chapter Eleven

HOW DO I GET TO THE HEART
OF THE MATTER?

*They go forth in it (the world) with well developed
bodies, fairly developed minds, and
undeveloped hearts.*
E. M. Forster

The young manager was thinking about his new responsibility. He had become more comfortable taking bigger risks with his staff. He had met with each of the managers individually and made sure: they agreed on the *form* needed for order with as much movement for freedom as possible; they had a safe place in which to create and work; they saw how their individual work was needed and meaningful in the big picture.

But there was still something missing. What held a group together? How could they create a form that would enable the team to work effectively with each other?

He decided to go for a walk.

Thankfully, he found Q. The young manager caught up with him.

"Good afternoon" he said falling into step.

"It is!" responded Q, "How is the new regional director doing on this fine day?"

"I'm glad you asked. All this talk about power killing learning, stifling growth and creating conformity in the team has made me a bit paranoid about my position. I know I need to have everyone work with me and I want order but I don't know how to put the final pieces together. We are doing much better, but there is something missing. We are like a team of horses who are headed in the right direction, but are pulling against each other. One manager protects 'his kingdom' against any intruder. Another is busy dumping and hiding her waste in places no one will look. Still another has a mouth that could stop a charging bull; he has nothing nice to say about anyone. What is it that that allow them to work with each other rather than against each other?"

"Good question. You are learning what you know and don't know and how to ask the right questions," began Q. He leaned over and whispered, "A little 'paranoia,' about your power is good." Q sat back. "The physical world has laws of cause and effect that determine what it does. Animals have instincts that guide them. They inherently know when to travel south, what to eat, when to sleep for the winter, run, jump or whatever it is that is written in their genes. But we are unique in all of creation. We are made in God's image. We have a free will. We can choose whether we will work together. Remember when I talked about values?"

"Yes, they are the basis for our choices," responded the young manager.

"Good," Q said. "It is our agreed-on core values that give us the ability to work together. God made us so that our freedom, and pursuing the most valuable choice, would be like a hand in a glove, working together. As values guide an individual, so they also provide the basis for how a group will work together. They are what will help a team pull together rather than against each other."

The young manager interjected, "Our core values are best defined for us by those things we feel strongest about, look after or listen for more than anything else."

"That's right," Q said as he nodded. "In fact, each of those areas we have talked about should function to reinforce and support the team's primary values. For instance, the reason you have a safe environment is so they can take risks and openly discuss assumptions and beliefs about sensitive issues. The reason you paint a clear picture is so they can see the value of where you are going. The reason you don't operate from power is so they can recognize the values for themselves and choose to invest themselves in their work without coercion."

The young manager's eyes grew big and he sat forward and said with excitement, "I see it! Common core values are the heart of any successful team. When you can bring the values - and their associated assumptions and beliefs - out into the open, agree to operate by them, and see them all woven into a clear and meaningful big picture, then you have a true learning system." He leaned back and said, "What happens if you don't have agreement on core values?"

Q leaned towards him and said, "Remember when we talked about form and freedom?"

"Yeah, *form* is the external structure needed to maintain order. Freedom is each person's unique expression of themselves in their work."

"Right," Q said. "When you agree on core values, you need less external *form*. When you differ on core values you need more external *form*."

The young manager thought for a moment, then said, "So if I can't get agreement on core values, I must create a *form* that will bring external order. I mean I would have to pay them more, give extra benefits or whatever to bribe them to do what I want or threaten them in some *form* to get them going?"

Q nodded his head and said, "Bribe and threat does create conformity, but shuts down almost all learning."

"How do I find our team values?" asked the young manager.

"In your team right now I will assume that you have never talked about your company's values?" Q asked.

"Not that I am aware of," the young manager replied.

"There are two areas you must look at. The first is a reminder and is tied back into the big picture of the company. Do you want product leadership? What you produce is the best on the market, period. Do you want to work in the middle providing the best price with the least inconvenience? Like a Wal-Mart. Do you want customer intimacy? Meaning you do everything possible to meet the customer's needs.[12] These are core values that will tie into vision."

The young manager shook his head. "Okay. We are working on those."

"Once you are all in tune with the company's values, then find the team values that will help get you there. These may include: clear communication, respect, justice, honesty, challenge, creativity, growth, support, or fun."

"But how could we do that as a team? Won't the values be different with each person?" asked the young manager.

"You can find core values to agree on. An important part is that you have opened the door for people to share. This allows you to understand different one's personal values and how to work with each other. Talk is easy when it comes to values, it is working them out that is the real challenge. When you create a system that can openly deal with values, then you can learn and change as you work with each other."

"Let's take one of my managers and walk through it together," the young manager said.

"Good idea," Q said.

"There's the sales manager. He has been kind of a pain lately. I think he secretly thought he should get my job and is fighting me the whole way."

"Okay," Q said. "You have read into his actions certain values he is operating under. Have you talked to him about this?"

The young manager looked at the teacher with humorous disbelief written all over his face.

"Talk to him about it? You're kidding, aren't you?"

"I'm not," Q said, "In our growing up we develop patterns of defensiveness whenever we are embarrassed or threatened. This defensiveness is to protect us from getting hurt or being vulnerable at the wrong time. It helps, but it can create problems when we need to work together and therefore learn and grow."

"How would you go about talking about values?" asked the young manager still in a daze at the thought.

"Let me ask you a question! Do you value him as an individual?" Q asked.

"Yes!"

Q interjected, "I mean, are you willing to work with him and develop a relationship of openness and honesty where apparent injustice can be talked about? Where the agreed upon values for the team and company are set forth by all? Where anyone not working in those values can be asked about his or her behavior? That includes that they can ask you hard questions as well."

"This sounds rather scary. I see the risk is that I may be questioned about my values. Isn't it easier to do business as usual?"

The young manager hesitated for a second and then said in mock seriousness with raised hands, "You know, play politics, blame others, scramble for power, stab people in the back and ... okay," he said with a grin, "I guess I've answered my own question. I don't like business as usual."

Q grinned and continued. "The stated value must truly be a value or he will see through it right away. If you truly value him and his input and want to be held accountable yourself to the value of justice, then it is possible to bring conflict out in the open. You have heard the old saying, 'Who you are is speaking so loud, I can't hear what you're saying.' We are all very perceptive. Even a child can see through a phony who proclaims one set of values and acts differently."

"You mean like one of those preachers who is caught with his pants down," responded the young manager.

"That's right. Some of them have told us how to act and yet do not model it. Their true values were shown by their actions. It is the same in your office as from a pulpit. Say what you mean, mean what you say."

"Any suggestions for defining our team values?" asked the young manager.

"Call the team together and explain what you want to do. The key in this is that you make available to them all the information you have, even the stuff that shows your warts. Leveling the playing field with common knowledge will speak louder than anything else that you are willing to trust them. Knowledge is power. If you give them knowledge, make all the facts known to them, then they can share the responsibility of interpreting it with you. Tell them what you know, what you think it means and then open it up for discussion.

"Once they see you are for real and the values are clarified and agreed upon based on knowledge everyone has, then procedures and policies are established to reflect those values. These procedures and policies become traditions and create an office culture. This creates congruency, which is what we are all seeking. Congruency in this case is when our behavior matches our values."

Q thought a moment and then added, "May I add a small note of caution here? Be careful not to judge the hearts of people. You are to concern yourself with behaviors that show values and are effective. A value can be expressed in different ways but with time, it is easy to agree or find research material to confirm that the behaviors do show the agreed upon values. If there are major attitude problems, send people to counselors."

Q smiled and said, "Over the last 15 years I have tried to work with my teachers in this way. Yes I have been hurt and used on occasion, but I don't regret it for a minute. When people are able to work from their heart, then they apply themselves and the work then becomes theirs. This ownership becomes a fertile soil for breeding creativity, risk, diligence and effectiveness. You have then created a place where transformational learning takes place, and in our changing world, that will be the only way to survive."

Silence hung in the air as both men pondered this challenging direction. Q, from experience, knew its worth. The young manager had begun to taste it, and realized looking ahead that the way was full of potential dangers, but he had already learned that risk was essential to anything good in life.

The young manager went back to work that day knowing he would take the risk.

LEARNING CELEBRATES:

<u>Values are at the heart of learning</u>.
Agreed on values allow freedom for individuals to express those values in their own unique way. Managers help staff understand their roles when they clarify expectations for their jobs and show how it fits into the big picture.

<u>When the environment is safe, people can deal with the roots of their ineffectiveness (The value set)</u>.
They can learn when their behavior is wrong or inappropriate. They grow stronger and become more effective when they learn.

<u>Values, when agreed on, produce order and after time produce traditions, customs and policies</u>.
The test for traditions, customs, policies and office culture is in how effectively they reflect the agreed upon values. Expressions of values may change, the core values of a business rarely do.

Chapter Twelve

HOW DOES IT FEEL?

"Do not imagine that if you meet a really humble man he will be what most people call "humble" nowadays: he will not be a sort of greasy, smarmy person, who is always telling you that, of course, he is nobody. Probably all you will think about him is that he seemed a cheerful, intelligent chap who took a real interest in what you said to him. If you do dislike him it will be because you feel a little envious of anyone who seems to enjoy life so easily. He will not be thinking about humility: he will not be thinking about himself at all."
C. S. Lewis

Several months passed and the young manager experienced the pleasure of working with what felt like a finely tuned orchestra. He felt comfortable in his job, it was the first time he was able to relax at work in years. He had even received a memo from the Vice President: 'good job.'

Most remarkably, he wasn't feeling the pressure to have to know everything. He could find out what he needed to know, by asking others or tapping into specialists he had found time to contact and ask questions. He also found great relief and empowerment in that he could accept change as a part of life and look forward to it bearing fruit as time progressed. He enjoyed taking new risks and there was a freshness in the air because of those risks. He was willing to take a look at things from different points of views, and to explore new areas before he made a decision. He even had extra time to catch a couple of his sons' baseball games.

In the past he hadn't felt "in control" over the office. But now, with his new skills, he realized that if he were not in control, it didn't mean everything was out of control. There was interconnected order and that was more fulfilling than power. His co-workers hammered out their team values and began to see changes in the office. His staff seemed friendlier, more of a functional family. They were allowing faults, and sharing some personal information as the days went on. Yet each knew what his or her part was and felt excitement and were challenged in reaching out to do it. He had lost a key player who asked to be transferred, but others rose to fill the spot.

The young manager stood up and looked out the window. Q sat feeding the pigeons. It was time for a visit to the little green bench.

The young manager smiled and said as he approached, "You are a popular person, you haven't given up feeding them, huh?"

"Not yet," Q said, "although I must confess I have retired the old 'hand trick,' but they are quite enjoyable, from a distance. You look like you are walking on cloud nine."

"I'm so happy with the way things are going at the office. I don't have any problems to talk about today. I had to come and express my gratitude and to tell you it's working," said the young manager with a smile, as he hugged the wise old teacher.

Q beamed and said, "Thanks. That means more than you can know." He paused, "You deserve most of the credit yourself. I only offered some simple thoughts I learned from children. You are the one who stepped up to the challenge and took the risks."

"With a teacher like you, how could I go wrong?" offered the young manager smiling.

They both sat and enjoyed the day and each other.

Q broke the silence and said, "I brought something for you to look at." He reached into his pocket and he pulled out an old tattered card and handed it to the young manager.

The young manager reached over and took it and looked at it.

"Is this my report card?" he said looking back at Q.

"No, it's the result of an IQ test given to a student years ago. Remember how I said you can't trust IQ tests? This is why. Look down there on the bottom. What does it say?"

The young manager held the old tattered paper closer.

"It says borderline mentally retarded."

Q nodded and said, "That's right. That's what they called that student."

The young student sensed a quietness he had not sensed before from Q. He leaned over and quietly asked, "Who was the student?"

Q leaned to meet his young student, smiled and whispered, "I was that student."

The young manager sat back in the bench and smiled.

Q shook his head slowly up and down as he looked over at his student and said, "That's right, those are my scores when I was young."

The young manager broke the silence and slowly began chuckling. Q joined him, and then the young manager started to laugh. Q launched out laughing harder and soon both of them were holding their sides. Minutes passed as they roared out loud together.

Finally Q spoke. "When you want to give up, when others try and put you in a box, when you're afraid of taking a risk, when you're misunderstood and you realize you're not bound by others, your only limit is what you're willing to reach out and take hold of. One thing I know, God made us able to do far more than we think we can."

The young student handed the tattered old paper back, "Thanks."

The young manager enjoyed the moment a little longer before adding, "Another manager called me yesterday and asked how I was getting such good reports."

He leaned over and said, "I told him I found a consultant who really knows what he is talking about."

Q smiled and said, "Oh you did, did you?"

The young manager smiled and said, "I did. I meet with him tomorrow to talk about it. Do you want to help him?."

"Hmmmm," said Q. "Tell you what I will do. You work with him and I will provide any support you need."

The young manager thought for a second and then said, "You're not going to let me off easy are you."

"I know," the young manager said, raising his hand, "challenge is good for learning."

Q nodded his head and smiled. "See you are ready to give what you know to someone else."

"Hey, wait a second," the young manager said, "What about that card you almost showed me on the first day? The one you said you kept with you to remind you of key things you had learned. I want to see that to compare what we have talked about with it."

Q reached in and pulled out the card and handed it to the young manager.
It read:

√ Ask questions -- even when you think you know.

√ Change can hurt, it involves our identity.

√ Find and instill values, they are the heart of the person.

√ Help them see the whole picture and what it means to them.

√ Provide a safe place to learn, encourage risk, learn from failure.

√ Find a form that fits; when in doubt, err on the side of freedom.

<u>Who I am is speaking so loud, they can't hear what I am saying.</u>

The young manager replied, "I think we did pretty good." He stood to leave and said, "I am looking forward to passing onto others what you have given to me. I will see you next week with my friend."

Q responded, "I will look forward to it and a chance to see you in action."

[1] Laing, R. D. (1970) <u>Knots</u>. New York: Pantheon p. 56

[2] Ornstein, R. & Thompson, (1984) <u>The Amazing Brain</u>

[3] Taylor, D. (1986) <u>The Myth of Certainty</u>, Grand Rapids, MI: Zondervan Publishing.

[4] Lewis, C. S. (1952) <u>Mere Christianity</u>, New York: MacMillan Publishing Co.

[5] Fisher, Kimball. (1993) <u>Leading Self-Directed Work Teams, A guide to developing new team leadership skills</u>, London: McGraw-Hill, Inc.

[6] Pearn, M., Roderick, C., Mulrooney, C. (1995) <u>Learning Organizations in Practice</u>. London: McGraw-Hill Book Company

[7] Fisher, Kimball. (1993) <u>Leading Self-Directed Work Teams, A guide to developing new team leadership skills</u>, London: McGraw-Hill, Inc.

[8] Caine, N. R., Caine G. (1991) <u>Making Connections: Teaching and the Human Brain</u>, Virginia: ASCD

[9] Bruya, B. (1994) Sunzi Speaks, <u>The Art of War</u>, Adapted & Illustrated by Tsai Chih Chung, Harper Collins Publishers,

[10] Caine, N. R., Caine G. (1991) <u>Making Connections: Teaching and the Human Brain</u>, Virginia: ASCD

[11] <u>Seven Habits of Highly Effective People</u>

[12] Treacy, M. & Wiersema, F. (1995) <u>The Discipline of Market Leaders</u>, Wokingham, England: Addison-Wesley Publishing Company

About the Author

Matt Rawlins works with the University of the Nations as a teacher and travels internationally as a trainer and consultant dealing with leadership and organizational issues.

With a Ph. D. in Philosophy, Matt has a heart to see people understand who they are and specifically, to help leaders communicate about difficult issues in times of change.

The author of six books, Matt is a gifted writer and communicator.

After living in Asia for ten years, he now resides with his wife Celia and son Joshua in Kailua-Kona, Hawaii.

You can contact him at:

mrawlins@hawaii.rr.com

CPSIA information can be obtained at www.ICGtesting.com
Printed in the USA
LVOW07s0919030115

421253LV00001B/8/P